TRANSPORTATION ISSUES, POLICIES AND R&D

SAFETY STANDARDS OF AUTOMOTIVE ELECTRONIC SYSTEMS

ISSUES AND ASSESSMENTS

TRANSPORTATION ISSUES, POLICIES AND R&D

Additional books in this series can be found on Nova's website under the Series tab.

Additional e-books in this series can be found on Nova's website under the eBooks tab.

TRANSPORTATION ISSUES, POLICIES AND R&D

SAFETY STANDARDS OF AUTOMOTIVE ELECTRONIC SYSTEMS

ISSUES AND ASSESSMENTS

MICHAEL J. HOLMES
EDITOR

New York

NOTICE TO THE READER

Library of Congress Cataloging-in-Publication Data

ISBN: 978-1-63485-908-0

Published by Nova Science Publishers, Inc. † New York

CONTENTS

PREFACE

On July 6, 2012, the President signed into law a new two-year transportation reauthorization bill, the Moving Ahead for Progress in the 21st Century Act (MAP-21.) This bill authorizes funds for Federal-aid highways, highway safety programs, transit programs, and for other purposes. This book responds to the MAP-21 requirement that the Secretary of Transportation to "complete an examination of the need for safety standards with regard to electronic systems in passenger motor vehicles." Moreover, the book reviews security and privacy gaps that put American drivers at risk.

In: Safety Standards of Automotive Electronic … ISBN: 978-1-63485-908-0
Editor: Michael J. Holmes

Chapter 1

ELECTRONIC SYSTEMS PERFORMANCE IN PASSENGER MOTOR VEHICLES*

National Highway Traffic Safety Administration

ACRONYMS

ACS	Accelerator Control System
ADAS	Advanced Driver Assistance Systems
AEB	Automatic Emergency Braking
Alliance	The Alliance of Automotive Manufacturers
ASC	The Automotive Safety Council
ASIL	Automotive Safety Integrity Level
AUTOSAR	AUTomotive Open System ARchitecture
CAFE	Corporate Average Fuel Economy
CAMP	Crash Avoidance Metrics Partners
CALCE	Center for Advanced Life-Cycle Engineering
CAN	Controller Area Network
CD/DVD	Compact Disk/Digital Video Disk
CDS	Crashworthiness Data System
CERT	Computer Emergency Response Team
CFR	Code of Federal Regulations
CIREN	Crash Injury Research and Engineering Network

* This is an edited, reformatted and augmented version of a Report to Congress, issued by the National Highway Traffic Safety Administration, December 2015.

CISS	Crash Investigation Sampling System
CMMI	Capability Maturity Model Integration
CRSS	Crash Report Sampling System
DARPA	Defense Advanced Research Projects Agency
DHS	Department of Homeland Security
DRBFM	Design Review Based on Failure Modes
DSRC	Dedicated Short Range Communications
ECU	Electronic Control Unit
EDR	Event Data Recorder
E/E	Electrical Electronic
EMC	Electro Magnetic Compatibility
EMI	Electro Magnetic Interference
ESC	Electronic Stability Control
ETC	Electronic Throttle Control
EVITA	E-safety Vehicle Intrusion Protected Applications
EWR	Early Warning Reporting
FAA	Federal Aviation Administration
FARS	Fatality Analysis Reporting System
FDA	Food and Drug Administration
FFA	Function Failure Analyses
FIPS	Federal Information Processing Standard
FMEA	Failure Mode and Effects Analysis
FMECA	Failure Modes, Effects, and Criticality Analysis
FMMEA	Failure Modes, Mechanisms, and Effects Analysis
FMVSS	Federal Motor Vehicle Safety Standard
FR	Federal Register
FTA	Fault Tree Analysis
GES	General Estimates System
Global	Association of Global Automakers
GM	General Motors
GPS	Global Positioning System
HACMS	High-Assurance Cyber Military Systems
HazOp	Hazard and Operability
HM-1	Health Management-1
IEC	International Electrotechnical Commission
IETF	Internet Engineering Task Force
IIHS	The Insurance Institute for Highway Safety
ISA	International Society for Automation
ISAC	Information Sharing and Analysis Center

ISO	International Organization for Standardization
IT	Information Technology
MAP-21	Moving Ahead for Progress in the 21st Century Act
MEMA	The Motor Equipment Manufacturers Association
MIL-STD	Military Standard
MISRA	Motor Industry Software Reliability Association
NAS	National Academies of Sciences
NASA	National Aeronautics and Space Administration
NASS	National Automotive Sampling System
NCAP	New Car Assessment Program
NHTSA	National Highway Traffic Safety Administration
NIST	National Institute of Standards and Technology
NRC	National Research Council
NTSB	National Transportation Safety Board
OBD-II	On Board Diagnostic
ODI	Office of Defects Investigation
OEM	Original Equipment Manufacturer
OTA	Over The Air
PBT	Performance-Based Test
PCI	Payment Card Industry
R2R	Resistor to Resistor
RESS	Rechargeable Energy Storage Systems
RF	Radio Frequency
RFC	Request for Comment
SCI	Special Crash Investigation
SDO	Standards Development Organization
SPICE	Software Process Improvement and Capability Determination
STPA	System Theoretic Process Analysis
TCG	Trusted Computing Group
TRB	Transportation Research Board
USB	Universal Serial Bus
VOQ	Vehicle Owner's Questionnaire

I. INTRODUCTION

On July 6, 2012, the President signed into law a new two-year transportation reauthorization bill, the Moving Ahead for Progress in the 21st

Century Act (MAP-21.) This bill authorizes funds for Federal-aid highways, highway safety programs, transit programs, and for other purposes.

Section 31402 of MAP-21, "Electronic Systems Performance" states that:

> "(a) IN GENERAL.—Not later than 2 years after the date of enactment of this Act, the Secretary shall complete an examination of the need for safety standards with regard to electronic systems in passenger motor vehicles. In conducting this examination, the Secretary shall—
>
> (1) consider the electronic components, the interaction of electronic components, the security needs for those electronic systems to prevent unauthorized access, and the effect of surrounding environments on the electronic systems; and
>
> (2) allow for public comment.
>
> (b) REPORT.—Upon completion of the examination under subsection (a), the Secretary shall submit a report on the highest priority areas for safety with regard to the electronic systems to the Committee on Commerce, Science, and Transportation of the Senate and the Committee on Energy and Commerce of the House of Representatives."

This report responds to the MAP-21 requirement that the Secretary of Transportation to "complete an examination of the need for safety standards with regard to electronic systems in passenger motor vehicles." [1] As outlined in section 31402, MAP-21 directed the agency to consider the following topics in conducting this examination:

1. electronic components,
2. interaction of electronic components,
3. security needs for those electronic components to prevent unauthorized access, and
4. effect of surrounding environments on the electronic systems.[2]

Moreover, MAP-21 directed the agency to allow for public comment in conducting this examination.[3] Upon completing the examination, MAP-21 also directed the agency to submit a report to Congress on the highest priority areas for safety with regard to the electronic systems.[4]

On October 7, 2014, the National Highway Traffic Safety Administration (NHTSA) issued a Request For Comment (RFC) in the Federal Register (FR) requesting public comment on Automotive Electronic Control Systems Safety and Security [Docket No. NHTSA-2014-0108[5]]. The RFC notice presented

NHTSA's progress thus far in conducting the "examination" referenced above as per required in section 31402. The RFC also illustrated how NHTSA is examining each of the areas described by Congress in section 31402 and sought public comment on the aforementioned examination. This report conveys NHTSA's findings from conducting its examination, addresses the public comments received from said examination, and subsequently lists "the highest priority areas for safety with regard to electronic systems."

II. BACKGROUND

The use of electronics in the design of modern automobiles is a rapid ongoing progression. The first common use of automotive electronics[6] dates back to the 1970s and by now a typical automobile features over 100 microprocessors, 50 electronic control units (ECUs), five miles of wiring and 100 million lines of code.[7] Use of electronics is not new. It has enabled safer and more fuel-efficient vehicles for decades. Electric and hybrid vehicles could not have been developed and produced without the extensive use of electronics, and proven safety technologies such as electronic stability control could not have been implemented. Over time, growth of electronics use has accelerated and this trend is expected to continue as the automotive industry develops and deploys even more advanced automated vehicle features. This trend results in increased complexities in the design, testing, and validation of automotive systems. Those complexities also raise general challenges in the areas of reliability, security, and safety assurance of increasingly networked vehicles leveraging electronics.

Electronics provide many safety, security, convenience, comfort, and efficiency functions for vehicle operators through interconnections and communications with other onboard electronics systems. Common communications networks and protocols allow for the exchange of information between sensors, actuators, and the ECUs that execute software programs to accomplish specific functions. A vehicle will typically feature multiple networks. Those networks may be isolated from one another for a variety of reasons such as safety and security; however, in other cases, different networks could be interconnected to enable exchange of information across a broader range of systems. Sharing data across multiple networks should be safeguarded against adverse influence over safety-critical systems; however, effectiveness of such approaches is only anecdotally known today. Growing system complexity and abundance of design variants, even within one manufacturer over model years and across classes of vehicles, potentially pose new safety and security challenges. Further, anomalies associated with electronic systems—including those related to software programming, intermittent electronics hardware malfunctions, and effects of electromagnetic disturbances—may not leave physical evidence, and hence are difficult to investigate without a record of data from the electronic systems.

While there are challenges, progressively introduced safety technologies, such as Automatic Emergency Braking (AEB), have the potential to significantly reduce the many thousands of fatalities and injuries that occur each year as a result of motor vehicle crashes. To that end, NHTSA recently announced that it plans to add two cutting-edge automatic emergency braking systems to the recommended advanced safety features included under the New Car Assessment Program (NCAP) – this latest step complements our half-century of regulating and promoting safety innovations. Our latest research shows that our regulatory program has saved 613,501 lives since 1960.[8] Further, continued innovation into more advanced forms of vehicle automation could address other types of crashes where human driver error plays a role. In May 2013, NHTSA released a preliminary statement of policy[9] concerning automated vehicles where the agency outlined its planned research into emerging technologies. Given the complexity of these new systems in terms of the additional electronics software and hardware needed, the safety of electronic control systems will continue to grow in importance as these systems become more commonplace in production vehicles. Increasingly advanced forms of automation may improve the overall safety of highways by addressing some of the common human driver errors, Even as the overall number of crashes are reduced, there may be a shift in the proportionality of accidents where the critical factor may be attributable to the drivers versus the equipment or the technology. These factors may necessitate future workforce adjustments to meet the technical and workload challenges that may be introduced into NHTSA's research, rulemaking, and defects investigation processes.

In 2010, the NHTSA funded a National Research Council (NRC) study on how the agency's regulatory, research, and defect investigation programs can be strengthened to meet the safety assurance and oversight challenges arising from the expanding functionality and use of automotive electronics. Proceedings of this research through the NRC-appointed 16-member committee is published in the Transportation Research Board (TRB) Special Report 308[10] by the National Academies of Sciences (NAS) in 2012 and identified five main challenges for the safety of future electronic control systems:

- An increased amount of complex software that cannot be exhaustively tested;
- The highly interactive nature of the electronic control system – more interactions exist among system components, and the outcome may be difficult to anticipate;
- The growing importance of human factors consideration in automotive electronic control system design;
- The potentially harmful interaction with the external environment including electromagnetic interference; and
- The novel and rapidly changing technology.

Further, the study offered recommendations to NHTSA on the actions that the agency could take to meet the five challenges referenced above. These include:

- becoming more familiar with and engaged in standard-setting and other efforts (involving industry) that are aimed at strengthening the means by which manufacturers ensure the safe performance of their automotive electronics systems;
- convening a standing technical advisory panel; undertaking a comprehensive review of the capabilities that the agency will need in monitoring for and investigating safety deficiencies in electronics-intensive vehicles;
- ensuring that Event Data Recorders (EDRs) become commonplace in new vehicles;
- conducting research on human factors issues informing manufacturers' system design decisions;
- initiating a strategic planning effort that takes into consideration the safety challenges resulting from vehicle electronics and that gives rise to an agenda for meeting them; and □ making the formulation of a strategic plan a top goal in NHTSA's overall priority plan.

In addition to the challenges regarding electronic components and their ability to function reliably in spite of their complex interactions, NHTSA believes there could also be increasing challenges with regard to the ability of these systems to remain free of unauthorized access or malicious attacks. While most of the documented demonstrations[11,12,13] of vehicle hacking to date have required some form of long-term physical access to the vehicle and the agency's review has not identified any reported real-world incidents resulting in a safety concern, the agency recognizes that lack of occurrence does not imply impossibility. In fact, security researchers recently demonstrated[14] the remote exploitation possibility with a passenger vehicle platform. NHTSA worked closely with the affected Original Equipment Manufacturers (OEMs) to identify and assess the risks and remedial solutions, which resulted in the affected OEM issuing a prompt voluntary recall (to implement a software patch) involving up to 1.4 million vehicles. The response to this incident also included an immediate step to mitigate long-range wireless vulnerabilities through an over-the-air update from the wireless service provider (with or without the software patch being applied to the affected vehicles). This event and subsequent actions were first of their kind and highlight the importance of maintaining particular vigilance for potential cybersecurity issues that have the potential to impact safety. NHTSA, via its RFC, also sought feedback from the public to determine what additional work is needed in this area. The findings will be discussed later in this report.

III. REVIEW OF SAFETY PROCESSES AND DATA SOURCES

III.1. Overview of Existing Safety Assurance Approaches

Notwithstanding the increased difficulty in the safety assurance of increasingly more complex systems, the automotive industry uses a number of safety standards and quality assurance practices in the design of safety-critical systems which are not unique to, but also cover, electronic systems. As documented in a number of publications and also summarized in the NAS Report, these approaches include the:

- establishment of system safety requirements;
- assessment of design hazards and risks at component, function, system, manufacturing and process levels such as by the use of failure mode and effects analysis[15] (FMEA) and fault tree analysis[16] (FTA);

- quality management systems such as ISO/TS 16949[17], advanced product quality planning, and Design for Six Sigma;
- design validation and verification testing such as electrical, environmental, laboratory, test track and limited field trials;
- variants of production part approval process; and
- post deployment field data analysis.

Further, many automotive original equipment manufacturers (OEMs) have been actively engaged in the development and revision of the ISO 26262[18] standard and most have already started to follow its principles.

III.2. Overview of Existing Safety Process Standards

Sectors of the automotive industry currently consider electronics safety and cybersecurity as part of its design and quality control processes. Three process standards from the broader transportation industry are frequently mentioned as suitable and preferred methods also used in the design of passenger vehicles usually complementing existing safety assurance practices:

1. ISO 26262 (Road Vehicles - Functional Safety): ISO 26262 is the first automotive industry specific standard[19] that addresses safety-related systems comprised of electrical, electronic, and software elements providing safety-related functions in the design of road vehicles. It is an adaptation to the International Electrotechnical Commission (IEC) 61508[20] standard to road vehicles. The first publication of ISO 26262 was in November 2011. This standard seeks to address various important challenges facing today's road vehicle technologies including:

- the safety of new electrical, electronic, and software functionality in vehicles;
- the trend of increasing system complexity, software content, and use of electromechanical components; and
- the risk from both systematic failure and random hardware failure.

Typical concerns associated with the ISO 26262 standard raised by industry stakeholder groups include:

- the standard could be laborious to apply;
- the hardware portions of the standard's coverage are very similar to existing industry practices with limited incremental benefits;
- the software portions of the standard primarily recommend good systems engineering practices for software safety; and
- the assessment of the automotive safety integrity levels (ASIL) may vary due to subjectivity in the process.

In part due to these limitations, existing practices and ISO 262626 are sometimes augmented with other system engineering approaches that are outlined in MIL-STD-882E and DO-178C, particularly on the software engineering side.

2. MIL-STD-882E (Department of Defense Standard Practice - System Safety): MIL-STD882E is the U.S. Department of Defense's systems engineering approach for eliminating hazards, where possible, and minimizing risks where those hazards cannot be eliminated. By taking a systems approach, this standard considers hazards in the entire lifecycle of systems, products, equipment, and infrastructure including design, development, test, production, use, and disposal stages. The principle of this standard is that system safety should follow the system engineering process, and is the responsibility of all functional disciplines, not just the system safety professionals. This standard has gone through a number of revisions in order to adapt to changes in technology and lessons learned through experience.

3. DO-178C (Software Considerations in Airborne Systems and Equipment Certification): In the aviation industry, DO-178C21 is an accepted guidance for showing compliance with the applicable airworthiness regulations related to the software development aspects of airborne systems and equipment certification. Conformance to this standard means the software satisfies airworthiness22 requirements with an acceptable level of confidence. As part of the airworthiness certification process, DO-178C provides guidelines to produce the software lifecycle data needed in order to support the certification process (e.g., plans for software development, verification, configuration management, and quality assurance). It also provides a comprehensive list of considerations in order to avoid errors and mistakes that could be introduced into software. DO-178C considers system software development as a subset of the overall system development process. It assumes that safety-critical requirements for software systems are defined in the higher-level system engineering activities and are given at the beginning of the

software development process. Some automotive companies indicated that the principles outlined in this more mature standard complement the software standard described in ISO 26262 Part 6,23 which is still evolving.

NHTSA continues to investigate functional safety approaches for the automotive industry that may effectively address emerging concerns from the increased use of electronics and software in the design of automobiles. The agency is also reviewing the following software-development standards/methodologies, which provide relevant guidance but were less commonly referenced by the automotive industry stakeholders:

- ISO/IEC 15504 - Automotive SPICE (Software Process Improvement and Capability Determination) and Capability Maturity Model Integration (CMMI): SPICE and CMMI are software process assessment models that provide a good strategy to assess organization's software development capability. They guide assessors to assign ratings to indicators and metrics in order to measure the capability of software processes.
- AUTomotive Open System ARchitecture (AUTOSAR): The objective of AUTOSAR is to create and establish open standards for automotive electrical/electronic architectures that will provide a basic infrastructure to assist with developing vehicular software, user interfaces, and management for all application domains. This includes the standardization of basic systems functions, scalability to different vehicle and platform variants, transferability throughout the network, integration from multiple suppliers, maintainability throughout the entire product life-cycle, and software updates and upgrades over the vehicle's lifetime.

NHTSA, via its RFC, sought feedback from the public to determine whether or not there were emerging gaps in the safety assurance processes of motor vehicles. The results will be discussed later in this report.

III.3. Overview of Available Data Sources

For purposes of determining the capabilities of various datasets to categorize and rank vehicle electronics safety issues, NHTSA considered vehicle recall data, vehicle owner's questionnaire (VOQ) data, early warning reporting (EWR) data, and data from its field crash databases the National

Automotive Sampling System (NASS), Fatality Analysis Reporting System (FARS), Crash Injury Research and Engineering Network (CIREN), and Special Crash Investigation (SCI) databases. Furthermore, EDR capabilities were also considered. Research findings on these various data sources are briefly described in this section. Although the agency feels that the sources of information available are useful in identifying the highest priority areas with regard to electronic components (and their interactions), it also believes that they have certain limitations in ranking safety issues associated with vehicle electronics. This limitation is mostly driven from the lack of detailed information regarding specific electronic system failure types.

The vehicle recall database[24] is a publicly available resource that documents safety defects or failures to meet minimum performance standards set by the Federal Motor Vehicle Safety Standards (FMVSS) in a motor vehicle or item of motor vehicle equipment. When manufacturers decide a safety defect or a noncompliance exists in a motor vehicle or item of motor vehicle equipment they manufactured, they are required to notify NHTSA and furnish a report with particular information about the defect or noncompliance, the products involved, and additional information including the manufacturer's plan to remedy for free the defect or noncompliance (See U.S.C. § 30118 and 49 CFR 573.6). Defect and noncompliance notifications and information reports are reviewed by NHTSA analysts who enter them in the recall database. The database includes summaries of the defect description, consequences, and remedy for each recall. The number of vehicle recalls has increased significantly in the past 20 years, more than tripling from 1993 (222) to 2014 (803). While the vehicle recall database contains a large amount of useful information, the database and underlying defect reports were not intended for detailed or precise statistical analyses of recalls by typology or root cause related to motor vehicle electronic systems. Any such analysis requires a manual review and classification process. However, this work can be limited by the amount of detail contained in the defect information reports that normally provide more general descriptions of the defect condition and potential safety consequences.

VOQs are voluntarily submitted by consumers to NHTSA to report a complaint in a vehicle or related equipment item. Each complaint (which is stored in a database and made available to the public redacted of personal identifiers) identifies the vehicle type, incident specifics, and includes a free form narrative to describe details. Complaint content and trends are helpful for general screening purposes but follow-up is sometimes necessary to verify and clarify complaints and incident specifics. Approximately 80,000 VOQs were filed in 2014.

The EWR system consists of several data types that are regularly reported to NHTSA by manufacturers. The data include non-dealer field reports (documents), listings of death/injury claims (records), and aggregated counts of certain claim types. The quarterly reporting interval, high-level component coding of aggregate figures, and variability in manufacturer reporting are factors that are considered when analyzing certain EWR data sets to study safety-critical embedded control systems. Field reports are the only EWR data sets available for evaluating specific defect conditions, including incidents in which the problem is intermittent or cannot be duplicated.

NHTSA also has multiple national crash databases. The NASS[25] is composed of two systems - the Crashworthiness Data System (CDS) and the General Estimates System (GES). Both of these systems are collect information from a nationally representative sample of motor vehicle crashes from sites across the country. The sample design is slightly different for each of these systems, but both have three stages of selections ending with a sample of police crash reports from across the country. Law enforcement officers complete crash reports for all crashes that meet their State's crash reporting criteria and NHTSA contractors access these reports in the selected sites, allowing NHTSA to make national estimates of crash characteristics. CDS data focus on passenger vehicle crashes involving at least one vehicle towed away post crash, and are used to investigate crash circumstances, vehicle crash response, and occupant injury and identify potential improvements in vehicle design. The Crash Investigation Sampling System (CISS) will replace CDS and is being phased in over the next few years. The CISS will add more pre-crash information to the dataset that has been historically featured in CDS, including better scene diagraming and more electronic data recorder data. The GES database contains crash statistics on close to six million police-reported crashes that occur annually involving all types of vehicles and all severities of crashes. Like the CDS, the information is collected from a sample of police reports. The GES will be replaced with an updated, though very similar system, the Crash Report Sampling System (CRSS), that will continue to collect overall information on crashes of all severities. Each NASS database is weighted to characterize a nationally-representative sample.

The FARS[26] database is a compilation of all fatal crashes in the United States containing similar information to NASS-GES. Through NHTSA/state cooperative agreements, state personnel populate the FARS database with information on the fatal crashes in their state. However, the FARS database also contains information from other state records in addition to the police crash report, such as driver's license, vehicle registration and coroner's reports. In both FARS and GES over 100 data elements that describe the crash are coded by trained data entry personnel; however, similar to the case with VOQs, there may be challenges in using these databases to perform detailed analyses for purposes of ranking emerging electronics concerns because the data elements were not established with this specific purpose in mind. In combination with other datasets, analysis of CDS, GES and FARS (and in the future CISS and CRSS) can still provide confirming or augmenting evidence in identifying potential priority areas in electronics reliability.

The CIREN database is created through NHTSA contracts/cooperative agreements and contains over 1,000 discrete fields of data concerning severe motor vehicle crashes, including crash reconstruction and medical injury profiles extending back to 1996. CIREN cases feature detailed data on occupant injury, vehicle damage and restraint technology and crash environment, as well as technical or human factors that are related to injury causation in motor vehicle crashes. Each CIREN case is reviewed by NHTSA contractors together with both medical and engineering professionals, along with the crash investigator, to determine injury causation and data accuracy.

The SCI[27] database contains a range of data collected by NHTSA contractors from basic crash data contained in routine police and insurance crash reports to comprehensive data from special reports by professional crash investigation teams. Hundreds of data elements relevant to the vehicle, occupants, injury mechanisms, roadway, and safety systems are collected for each of the over 100 crashes designated for study annually. The SCI case selection criteria are set based on NHTSA priority interests and can change through-out the year. SCI cases are intended to be an anecdotal data set useful for examining special crash circumstances or outcomes from an engineering perspective. The SCI program's flexibility allows for investigations of new emerging technologies related to automotive safety.

Finally, EDRs[28] are devices that may be installed in a motor vehicle to record technical vehicle information for a few seconds leading up to the crash. For instance, EDRs may record vehicle speed, engine throttle position, brake use, driver safety belt status, and air bag warning lamp status. NHTSA has been using EDRs to support its crash investigation program for several years and EDR data are routinely incorporated into NHTSA's crash databases. This type of data could potentially play a role in finding when safety-critical automotive electronics were not functioning properly.

NHTSA, via its RFC, sought feedback from the public as to what other sources of information and data are available. The results will be discussed later in this report.

IV. EXAMINATION OF THE NEED FOR AUTOMOTIVE SAFETY STANDARDS

NHTSA has been actively engaged in research (both internally and with outside parties) in automotive electronics reliability, cybersecurity, and emerging technologies in advanced vehicle automation for the past two years. The agency has established, per MAP-21,[29] a Council on "Vehicle Electronics, Vehicle Software, and Emerging Technologies" to coordinate and share information on a broad array of topics related to advanced vehicle electronics and emerging technologies. The Council is comprised of NHTSA staff and governed by senior NHTSA management. The mission of the group is to (1) broaden, leverage, and expand the agency's expertise in motor vehicle electronics to continue ensuring that technologies enhance vehicle safety, and (2) review and advice on the research program established over electronics reliability, cybersecurity, and automation topics.

With input from the Council, NHTSA has identified and funded initial research into the following areas:

- Hazard analyses of safety-critical electronic vehicle control systems that govern vehicle motion, applying Hazard and Operability (HazOp) process referenced within the ISO 26262 standard as well as System Theoretic Process Analysis (STPA);
- Examination of process-oriented functional safety and security standards for automotive electronics design and development;
- Automotive cybersecurity concerns, threats, vulnerabilities, and potential countermeasures;
- Best practices in safeguarding against cybersecurity risks in related but in non-automotive industries; and
- Human factors and other emerging concerns associated with highly automated vehicles.

Because NHTSA was already investigating vehicle electronics as a new and emerging research area for vehicle safety prior to the passage of MAP-21, the agency has already completed some research and analyses that address some of the items listed by Congress in section 31402 of MAP-21. Research reports are available on the agency's website[30] and it is expected that more reports will be published as projects are completed over the 2015-2016 timeframe. It should be noted that the research described in this report represents research already underway and future research that the agency anticipates undertaking as resources permit.

The following sections (IV.1 – IV.3) present the agency's initial progress on the areas that Congress directed the agency to consider in the examination required under section 31402. Subsequently, NHTSA, via its RFC, sought feedback from the public on the issues identified in this section. The results will be discussed later in this report.

IV.1. Electronics Components and the Interaction of Electronic Components

To examine the potential safety concerns associated with electronic components and interactions of electronic components, NHTSA initiated research in developing potential approaches to analyzing the automotive electronic control system architecture and its interconnections. In conjunction, the agency reviewed data sources available to NHTSA to assess the datasets that would be useful to analyze for purposes of this initiative. Further, the agency initiated systematic hazard analyses on select safety-critical automotive control systems to better understand the vehicle level safety risks. In the following paragraphs, further details are provided on these research topics, enabling an initial, systematic examination of the first two areas stated in MAP-21.

NHTSA is also conducting research to develop an electronics-related failure-typology.[31] As part of this research, the agency is evaluating the various sources of data (e.g., defect data, crash databases, etc.) to determine if suitable data exist at this time to effectively utilize a detailed failure typology that would describe and categorize the hazards and causes of automotive electronic control system failures. Through such analysis, the agency would like to understand how trends in the underlying data for the chosen dataset change over time as a function of increased use of electronics. NHTSA plans to complete and publish its initial failure-typology research in 2016. If new datasets are identified or become available, the agency may perform follow-up studies in the future.

The agency is also studying the automotive electronic system architecture. Functional safety assurance of modern automobiles requires a thorough understanding of electronic control systems' design under a variety of scenarios. These circumstances include systems' behavior under nominal conditions and also during failure conditions. Equally important are state-of-the-art capabilities in detecting failures (diagnostic/prognostic) and fault-tolerant and/or fail-safe strategies that can prevent errors from resulting in safety hazards. To this end, NHTSA funded initial research to perform hazard analyses in select safety-critical automotive control system areas, such as Accelerator Control Systems (ACS)/Electronic Throttle Control (ETC), Rechargeable Energy Storage Systems (RESS), and steering and braking control systems within the context of automatic lane centering function. These studies apply the HazOp process referenced within the ISO 26262 standard as well as the STPA approach to identify the system-level hazards and causal factors associated with potential failures in the subject control systems. The purpose of these studies is to better understand the critical automotive system functions, failures, and risks and identify safety goals and requirements. Further, another purpose is to compare and contrast results obtained from existing hazard analyses techniques. The agency is currently prioritizing its hazard analysis research to cover electronic throttle control, steering control, braking control, and motive power areas. It intends to publish a series of research reports on hazard analyses starting in 2016.

A typical automotive electronic control system primarily relies on the following to perform its intended purposes:

- Sensors (measurements);
- Interpretation of sensed signals (e.g., conversion, configuration, classification);
- Estimations of parameters (when direct sensing may not be available, e.g., vehicle speed);
- Actuators (to carry out the intended motive);
- Communication networks (that facilitate electronic exchange of information between sensors, controllers, and actuators);
- Design and programming of the control algorithm (conditions and respective actions) including:
    - design and software coding that implement:

        - the intended functions and
        - system monitoring and malfunction detection logic; and
    - supervisory logic that arbitrates between multiple, potentially conflicting, subsystem commands; and
- Availability and management of motive power.

Interactions between electronic components (and distributed embedded systems) are facilitated primarily by communication networks and shared use of sensors, software logic, and actuators. Prioritization of competing requests from the various control subsystems and the driver for safety-critical functions is a potential area of anticipated future research due to continued proliferation of automotive safety and convenience functions.

IV.2. Security Needs to Prevent Unauthorized Access to Electronic Components

NHTSA defines cybersecurity, within the context of passenger vehicles, as the protection of vehicular electronic systems, communication networks, control algorithms, software, users, and underlying data from malicious attacks, damage, unauthorized access, or manipulation.

NHTSA has been actively researching existing cybersecurity standards, guidelines and best practices in government agencies (e.g., the Food and Drug Administration (FDA), Federal Aviation Administration (FAA), Department of Homeland Security (DHS), Department of Commerce etc.) and industry (e.g., the automotive OEMs and suppliers, etc.). In reviewing the practices of other industries in dealing with cybersecurity issues, NHTSA has identified two general process-oriented approaches that are commonly cited as beneficial towards addressing cybersecurity concerns:

1. Design and quality control processes that focus on cybersecurity issues throughout the lifecycle of a product.
2. Establishing robust information sharing forums such as an Information Sharing and Analysis Center (ISAC).

In regards to security design and quality assurance processes, the automotive manufacturers, suppliers, and other stakeholders are collaborating through SAE International to examine the emerging vehicle cybersecurity concerns and considering actions that could include the development of voluntary standards, guidelines, or best practices.

While there may be no readily-available automotive cybersecurity standards at the time this report was prepared, NHTSA's research identified general cybersecurity safeguarding approaches that can potentially be examined and adapted for use in the automotive industry. For example, the cybersecurity framework[32] developed and published by the National Institute of Standards and Technology (NIST) treats cybersecurity as a process integrated into the system, component, and device lifecycle. The guidelines referenced in this framework might allow the automotive industry to develop a security program for modern-day automobiles analogous to information security programs in place for information technology (IT) systems in general. Similarly, system security engineering could potentially be incorporated into the design process in a way similar to system safety engineering as specified in ISO 26262 and "E-safety vehicle intrusion protected applications (EVITA)."[33]

In regards to information sharing mechanisms, NHTSA studied[34] the ISAC model for safeguarding against cybersecurity risks and threats in other industries such as financial services, information technology, and communications. The initial analyses indicate that an automotive sector specific information sharing forum, such as an ISAC, is beneficial to pursue. It could advance the cybersecurity awareness and countermeasure development effectiveness among public and private stakeholders. ISACs have a unique capability to provide comprehensive inter- and intra-sector coverage to share critical information pertaining to sector analysis, alert and intelligence sharing, and incident management and response. Discussions with technical experts across various industries, as well as our Federal partners, indicate that total prevention of cyberthreats would be a difficult task. The successful use of ISACs in other industry sectors suggest that it might also be effective for the auto industry to have mechanisms in place to expeditiously exchange information related to cyber-threats, vulnerabilities, and countermeasures among industry stakeholders. Such a mechanism would enhance the ability of the automotive sector to prepare for, respond to, and recover from cyber threats, vulnerabilities and incidents. Related to the sector-wide cybersecurity information sharing topic, the Alliance of Automotive Manufacturers (Alliance) and the Association of Global Automakers (Global Automakers) wrote[35] to NHTSA in July 2014 to inform about the new cybersecurity initiative they are undertaking with the goal of establishing a voluntary automobile industry sector ISAC or other comparable program. In response[36], NHTSA encouraged the Alliance and Global Automakers (as well as automotive OEMs) to proceed expeditiously with the outlined process and expressed the agency's hope that their plan would target a date in 2015 for an automotive industry ISAC to become operational. Upon completing their study on the specifications for the ISAC needed for the automotive sector, in July 2015, Alliance and Global announced that the industry is moving forward with voluntarily developing and launching an Auto ISAC and that they expect the entity to begin operations by late 2015.

Security process standards and information sharing forums fit in a larger, more comprehensive automotive cybersecurity assurance approach. In general terms, there are four major pieces to the agency's research approach:

1. Protective/Preventive methods and techniques: This group of techniques would seek to harden the design of automotive electronic systems and networks such that it would be difficult for malicious attacks to take place in newer generation systems. Deployment and use of structured security process standards could help identify vulnerabilities such that necessary design improvements can be identified and implemented. These vulnerabilities include possible entry points through accessible physical interfaces such as the On-Board Diagnostic (OBD)-II port, Universal Serial Bus (USB) ports, CD/DVD players; short range wireless interfaces, such as Bluetooth, Wi-Fi, or Dedicated Short Range Communications (DSRC); and long-range wireless interfaces such as cellular or satellite-based connectivity to the vehicle. Examples of design improvements include potential use of:

a. encryption and/or authentication on communication networks;
b. different communication approaches, architectures or protocols;
c. segmentation/isolation of safety-critical system control networks;
d. redundant communications, direct measurements, message authentication, source validation for safety-critical system inputs;
e. strong authentication controls for remote access vectors to vehicles;
f. gateway controls and firewalls between interfaced vehicle networks;
g. formal methods[37] for the specification, development and validation of embedded systems; etc.

The primary intents of this category of activities are 1) to significantly reduce the probability of cyber risks, and 2) to limit the impacts of a potential cybersecurity breach (e.g., one part of one vehicle or just one vehicle as opposed to a fleet of vehicles). NHTSA initiated applied research into vulnerability assessment and preventive type measures in 2014 and expects to publish reports starting in 2016.

2. Real-time intrusion detection methods: Total security through preventive measures may not be realistically achievable. Thus, as a complement to the preventative measures, detecting intrusions into the system through communications networks could provide additional protection. A cybersecurity breach could take place on or through a communication network. From an intrusion detection perspective, vehicular network communications are considered fairly predictable and well-suited for real-time monitoring to detect anomalous activity with respect to nominal expected message flows. The agency is initiating research into this type of technologies in the automotive sector.
3. Real-time response methods: Once a potential intrusion is detected, the strategies to mitigate its potential harmful impacts would also need to be designed in a practical manner. Depending on the potential risks and level of intrusion detection confidence, the vehicle architecture could be designed to take a variety of actions such as: temporarily or permanently shut down the communication network(s) (at the potential cost of disabling various safety functions); inform the driver; record and transmit data before-and-after the trigger point for further analysis and counter-measure development; etc. The purpose of this category of cybersecurity defense is to mitigate the potential harmful consequences of detected anomalous activity on the vehicle experiencing the potential breach. The agency expects to develop further research into this category of methods in 2016.
4. Treatment methods: While the previous paragraph discussed response methods (deal with ensuring fail-safe operation of the vehicle where an intrusion is detected), treatment methods deal with distributing information related to the subject risk to other potential vulnerable entities before the compromise may be experienced by others. Treatment methods involve timely information extraction from impacted parties, their analysis, development of countermeasures and timely dissemination to all relevant stakeholders (such as through an ISAC). This approach allows for design of stronger preventive methods in future generations of electronics. As outlined earlier, the automotive industry (through Alliance and Global Automakers) is

actively exploring information sharing alternatives related to automotive cybersecurity, and NHTSA is closely monitoring activities related to this initiative.

Related to the topic of automotive cybersecurity, Senator Edward J. Markey sent letters to major automobile manufacturers in December 2013 requesting information about how their consumers are protected from cyberattack and unwarranted violations of privacy. Later, in February 2015, Senator Markey's office released a report[38] based on OEM responses. In this report, Senator Markey recommends that NHTSA, in consultation with the Federal Trade Commission (FTC) on privacy issues, promulgate new standards that will protect the data, security and privacy of drivers in the modern age of increasingly connected vehicles. Further, the report suggests that such standards related to cybersecurity should include the following considerations, which are consistent with and are elements of NHTSA's research areas outlined above:

- Ensure that vehicles with wireless access points and data-collecting features are protected against hacking events and security breaches;
- Validate security systems using penetration testing; and
- Include measures to respond real-time to hacking events.

IV.3. Effects of the Surrounding Environment on Electronic Component Performance

In addition to malicious interference that may be artificially introduced (as covered under cybersecurity in section IV. 2.), the surrounding natural environment could affect the electronic components and systems in three primary ways by creating conditions:

1. that could cause electronic components to fail prematurely;
2. that could result in electronic control systems to act in unintended ways; and
3. for electronic sensors or systems to perceive the environment differently than reality.

Effects of the environment potentially causing electronic components to fail prematurely, such as through moisture, heat, and corrosion are typically handled by fail-safe strategies. Monitoring algorithms can detect sensors and components that fail and operate outside of the intended range and inform control algorithms to operate in fail-safe mode. Manufacturers take placement and environmental exposure into account in the design of electromechanical components.

Examples of the environment potentially causing electronic control systems to act in unintended ways are electromagnetic interference (EMI) and potential build-up of low-resistance paths on a circuit-board, such as a tin whisker.[39] OEMs very commonly perform electromagnetic compatibility (EMC) testing on their platforms in accordance with SAE International[40] and ISO[41] standards. NHTSA has investigated EMI effects on an electronic control system in a recent investigation. In 2010, NHTSA and the National Aeronautics and Space Administration (NASA) conducted EMC testing as part of the inquiry into whether or not unintended acceleration was related to the electronic throttle control system in Toyota vehicles. In this study, EMC testing at exposure levels well above existing certification standards did not produce open throttle.[42] Among the risks with EMI is for the ECU's memory settings to be altered unintentionally. This could change the way the system behaves especially if the EMI's influence is not detected. Manufacturers utilize various methods to prevent unintended EMI influence, such as by retaining safety-critical system parameters in more than one memory location (such that a random alteration could be detected and system shut down with warning).

Formation of conductive tin whiskers on a circuit board could potentially result in low-resistance paths and unintended system behavior, particularly if they cause a short between circuits resulting in unintended activation of an actuator. Most such issues result in electrical faults and safe shut-down of corresponding functions. Manufacturers use various techniques to mitigate the concern including changes to the manufacturing process, addition of elements like copper and nickel, and the use of surface coatings. Further, circuit board design takes into account the possibility of circuit board shorts in trace placement.

Another possibility is for the environment to impact the advanced sensors (such as radar, LIDAR, cameras, GPS, etc.) on a contemporary vehicle in a way that could result in unintended engagement or non-operational status of system functions. To mitigate this risk, manufacturers utilize various forms of sensor fusion technologies to reduce reliance on any single sensor signal for safety-critical functions.

Related to 5.9 gigahertz (GHz) band in the DSRC, NHTSA is initiating research into analyzing potential communication interference impacts of devices that operate on and in neighboring spectrums of the DSRC band[43]. NHTSA expects to complete this study in 2016.

V. PUBLIC COMMENTS AND RECOMMENDATIONS

NHTSA issued an RFC on October 7, 2014, on the safety and security of automotive electronic control systems. The comment period ended on December 8, 2014. The RFC provided the public with the information summarized in Sections II, III, and IV of this document, and solicited comments and responses from the public on 37 questions or question clusters (see Appendix A) from among the following four topic areas:

1. Electronics Components and the Interaction of Components
2. Security Needs to Prevent Unauthorized Access to Electronic Components
3. Effects of the Surrounding Environment on Electronic Component Performance
4. Additional Comments

The purpose of the RFC questions was to gain specific feedback on these topics, which include inquiries about NHTSA's current research approach and requests for existing safety and security standards as described in Sections III and IV. Any further general comments of particular interest are noted separately.

A total of 40 organizations and individuals responded44 to the RFC by submitting 53 documents. Some of these documents provided either duplicate, background, or supporting information. A detailed breakdown of the respondents and summary of their comments are provided in Appendix B.

Broadly, RFC responses supported NHTSA's research platform as a foundation that can be further strengthened to improve vehicle safety and security in the context of increasingly complex system interactions. The respondents provided comments and recommendations that identified some additional opportunities for consideration in future research and activities by NHTSA. Public recommendations and NHTSA responses will be discussed with further details in this section.

V.1. Electronic Components and the Interaction of Electronic Components

For this topic, the public made the following recommendations to NHTSA in six areas:

1. RFC Response Summary for Safety Analysis of Priority Control Systems

The respondents concurred that NHTSA should continue research of electronic control systems impacting steering, braking propulsion, and motive power. They also suggested that this approach can be further strengthened by including additional systems that interact with these fundamental motion control functions. The RFC response comments emphasize this approach because vehicle systems' relationship to fundamental vehicle controls is mentioned to be not always obvious. Examples of such systems and sensors of interest suggested by respondents include:

- Advanced driver assistance systems (ADAS) (AAA, Delphi, and Micron)
- Airbag and restraint systems (AAA, Bosch, Denso, and The Insurance Institute for Highway Safety (IIHS))
- Electric vehicle engine/powertrain monitors - current sensors, temperature (Automotive Safety Council (ASC), Bosch, and Delphi)
- Battery controls (Bosch)
- Vehicle lighting controls and other visibility aids; Automatic light control systems (Delphi and Denso)
- Impact sensors for pedestrian protection (ASC and Delphi)
- Engine management sensors (ASC and Delphi)
- Temperature sensors (ASC and Delphi) - especially those used for over-temperature shutoff, with safety relation, etc.
- Driver assistance; i.e., interaction and/or override of driver commands (Delphi)
- Driver state monitoring – drowsy, distracted, head pose, eye gaze (Delphi)
- Automatic wiper systems (Denso)
- Suspension control systems (General Motors (GM))
- Transmission control (GM)

- Pedestrian detection sensors (ASC)
- Active safety sensors (ASC and GM)

IIHS and ASC strongly argued to research safety restraint systems in conjunction with impacts to fundamental motion control functions and posited that they are not mutually exclusive. Whereas one can impact collision outcomes, the other impacts collision frequency; hence, they recommend parallel research.

NHTSA response: The RFC responses indicated that many automotive systems and electronics are safety-related. As the agency assigns highest priority to researching electronic control systems that directly impact fundamental motion controls, it is exploring methods of categorizing additional research needs in this area. The agency's prioritization of fundamental motion controls is broadly supported by the public. NHTSA will move toward the analysis of other safety-relevant systems (e.g., ADAS, airbag and restraint systems, and others listed above) within the constraints of its resources as agency-research goals and the next round of priorities are determined.

2. RFC Response Summary for Hazard Analysis Approaches

Various respondents suggested that NHTSA should implement newer approaches to hazard identification such as STPA and consider other tools in addition to HazOp. It is suggested that methods which complement HazOp could include:

- Function Failure Analysis (FFA) (Delphi)
- FTA (Continental, Denso, and Schaeffler)
- Failure Modes, Mechanisms and Effects Analysis (FMMEA) (Diganta Das with Center for Advanced Life-Cycle Engineering (CALCE) at University of Maryland and Bhanu Sood)
- Motor Industry Software Reliability Association (MISRA) systems safety analysis (Delphi)
- Design Review Based on Failure Modes (DRBFM) (Denso)
- Argumentation structures/causal reasoning (William Scherlis at Carnegie-Mellon University)
- Human Factors research to explore hazards associated with driver related challenges such as fatigue and distraction (Ford)

On the other hand, Continental and Schaeffler cautioned the agency stating that methods lacking clear methodological definitions (e.g., STPA) may not be suitable to ensure comprehensible or reproducible results needed by OEMs to meet regulations referring to international standards in other countries. Schaeffler further stated that it does not see a need for, or a benefit from, alternative approaches for hazard and risk assessment citing potential complication and additional unreasonable effort for global suppliers during the product development process.

NHTSA response: As outlined in the FR notice, the agency is currently applying STPA as a complement to the HazOp study referenced in the ISO 26262 standard. The purpose of agency's approach is not to compare and contrast various hazard analysis tools, but to gain insights into their uses in an applied setting. Additionally, NHTSA has researched FTA, FMEAs, and MISRA as well as variants and extensions of FMEAs, such as FFA and Failure Modes, Effects, and Criticality Analysis (FMECA) and acknowledges the recommendations to look into other methods such as DRBFM, and FMMEA. NHTSA is interested in exploring any analysis technique that could improve hazard identification and mitigation. Other complementary approaches will be analyzed as agency research goals are reviewed and revised, and as resources permit. It is agreed that well-defined processes that deliver repeatable and reproducible results are essential.

NHTSA is pursuing a broad range of activities regarding human factors research. The agency is researching the industry practices for communicating system and error states to drivers in each of its functional safety research topics. The agency is also incorporating STPA as part of its hazard analysis process, which includes the assessment of potential system-level failures associated with a human driver action or inaction. These methods are being applied to accelerator, brake, steering, and power management control systems. The agency also recognizes human factors as one of the most challenging and important areas of research for safe operation of highly automated vehicles. As a result, the agency's automation research program features various human factors projects to better understand driver behavior, use, misuse, and potential abuse of automated vehicles as well as vehicle- and traffic-level hazards that may be caused or introduced by them.

3. RFC Response Summary for Safety Assurance Processes

RFC respondents broadly supported the ISO 26262 standard as an effective approach to evaluate hazards and risks of automotive control systems, but limitations were noted, some to be addressed with the next version of the standard, others requiring complementary approaches. Bosch, Delphi, GM, SAE International, Trusted Computing Group (TCG) and TRW indicated that several standards are available that could address electronic component and security concerns not addressed by voluntary safety process standards, including updated ISO 26262, Internet Engineering Task Force (IETF) RFC 2196, International Society for Automation (ISA)/IEC 62443, NIST's Federal Information Processing Standard (FIPS), and Payment Card Industry (PCI) security standards. TRW noted that it is difficult to establish mandatory requirements for ISO 26262's utilization. The standard addresses aspects of product development that necessarily vary depending on specific application and safety goals under development, and thus its application not necessarily leads to unique outcomes. Still, Bosch noted ISO 26262 offers improved system understanding, better cooperation between OEM and supplier, and unified/structured language and process; but the standard –to some extent– is open for interpretation, particularly leading to different assessments of the ASILs for some functions. TRW indicated NHTSA could provide data to objectively determine the ASIL and therefore ameliorate subjectivity in this effort. It was suggested that NHTSA should strengthen ISO 26262's role as a process standard through influencing the revision of this standard and use of the complementary approaches described above. Further, Alliance, Delphi, Ford, Global, and Mercedes-Benz requested that NHTSA collaborate within existing standards forums (e.g. ISO and SAE committees) to further refine/apply ISO 26262.

On a more general note, the respondents suggested that NHTSA develop industry standards through partnerships rather than trying to develop new standards that may not be effective across all vehicle components. Further, they asked NHTSA to

i. collaborate among government, existing industry and voluntary standards organizations, and academia (Delphi, Global, and Ford);
ii. convene regular forums for the broader industry to review NHTSA's research plan and outcomes so stakeholders can provide timely input to address potential gaps and collaborate within existing standards forums to develop practical solutions (Mercedes-Benz and Alliance).

Alliance cautioned NHTSA to avoid specifying standards based on today's technology that might have the unintended consequence of hindering future technological advances. Delphi stated that the best approach is continued development of industry standards with a guidelines approach that looks at high-level requirements. Similarly, the Motor Equipment Manufacturers Association (MEMA) stated that any mandated standard development is premature and urges NHTSA to consider guidance development instead. MEMA further stated that such an approach could provide a build-up to potential future requirements while providing a foundation upon which to build experience and practical application. Finally, respondents were divided in their views on whether existing process standards are suitable to address electronic control system design challenges for more advanced forms of vehicle automation.

NHTSA response: NHTSA concurs with the stated importance of collaborating with industry, standards-development organizations (SDOs), and academia to develop standards that ensure the safety and security of automotive electronic systems. In fact, the agency is currently a very active participant in committees regarding functional safety, cyber security, and automation. It has representatives that serve as liaisons on the following SAE committees:

a. Functional Safety Committee
b. Vehicle Electrical System Security Committee
c. On-Road Automated Vehicle Standards Committee

In addition to the three main committees listed above, the agency also has representatives serving on the following SAE committees:

a. HM-1 Integrated Vehicle Health Management Committee
b. On-Road Automated Vehicle Safety Testing Task Force
c. On-Road Automated Vehicle Planning Task Force
d. Vehicle Electrical/Electronic (E/E) System Diagnostic Standards Committee
e. Battery Standards Electronic Fuel Gauge Committee
f. Future Parameters for J1698 Task Force

NHTSA's commitment to collaboration is further demonstrated by the agency's cooperative research with the Crash Avoidance Metrics Partnership (CAMP), its continued involvement with SAE International, and its ongoing research collaboration with university research centers.

As referenced previously in section III.3 of this report, NHTSA's approach to setting "minimum safety standards" is performance-based, which allows for innovation and future technological advances.

NHTSA agrees that functional safety and cybersecurity research can be integrated to get a more comprehensive understanding of electronic components, potential hazards, and associated residual risks in making design decisions. While conventional design-for-safety approaches consider random or natural failures and their associated likelihoods in determination of residual risks, cybersecurity considerations also introduce the risks of potential artificial introduction of failure conditions. Therefore, the agency continues to study the benefits of placing cybersecurity early in the development process in conjunction with functional safety. Early consideration of cybersecurity could lead to design choices which mitigate hazards even though traditional analysis methods may view the residual risks associated with natural failures acceptable. An integrated security/functional safety process may be able to influence design approaches that could address potential safety ramifications of cybersecurity hacks associated with the safety-critical control systems.

4. RFC Response Summary for Performance-based Tests

The RFC responses suggested that NHTSA develop guideline methodologies (e.g., being developed by SAE's Automotive Security Guidelines and Risk Management Committees) that focus on high-level functional requirements and safety goals, taking into consideration interrelated functional safety processes so that system-level performance-based tests (PBTs) can be derived from these principles in collaboration with the OEMs through forums such as CAMP. Ford and SAE International supported this approach. On the other hand, Delphi stated that PBTs would not 'ensure' safety on their own. Delphi further stated that any test should be against a requirement; therefore, PBTs would require a set of functional and safety requirements that would be expected to be a subset of the complete set of requirements (component level and system level.) Evidence from other phases of development would be needed to confirm safe-operation with regards to all factors causal to harm. In addition, the RFC respondents requested that NHTSA determine performance criteria at the system or vehicle level, not at the component level. Further, Continental, Ford, GM, and SAE International expressed concerns over generic PBTs, noting, for example, that variation among products (manufacturer-specific tuning and implementation variations) makes it difficult to normalize results; and that PBTs are very application-specific.

NHTSA response: The agency agrees that, consistent with its current practices, any potential performance criteria associated with functional safety or cybersecurity requirements would likely be set at the system or vehicle level. Lower-level subsystem and component requirements can be driven from these higher-level criteria, which may vary based on the electrical/electronic architecture and proprietary approaches used on a given vehicle platform. The agency acknowledges the public feedback that safety assurance through a manageable number of PBTs could be difficult.

Related to cybersecurity specifically, due to the highly-dynamic nature of cybersecurity risks and threats, NHTSA recognizes that setting minimum performance criteria and performance-based tests could be a challenge without the risk of becoming outdated quickly. NHTSA has been in discussions with the industry and other government agencies[45] on potential effective approaches to address cybersecurity. Further, the agency continues to actively follow SAE International's Vehicle Electrical System Security Committee activities toward developing the J3061[46] Cybersecurity Guidebook for Cyber-Physical Automotive Systems. The development of robust cybersecurity guidelines among the agency alternatives has not only been widely supported, but is also one approach being pursued by other Federal Agencies[47] to address cybersecurity risks.

5. RFC Response Summary for Diagnostics, Prognostics, and Fail-safe Strategies

The RFC respondents suggested that NHTSA should collect diagnostic and failure data from both restraint systems and crash avoidance or mitigation systems to capture a more comprehensive understanding of control system interactions. Further, they recommended NHTSA to work with automotive OEMs to develop a standardized monitoring architecture for diagnostics and prognostics, including plausibility checks, software function monitoring, processor hardware monitoring, and communication end-to-end checks. GM stated that prognostics should be the last area to pursue for safety benefits compared to vehicle health management and diagnostics. Related to fail-safe considerations, Bosch suggested that NHTSA should explore the possibility of a cyber-physical attack potentially preventing a system from reaching a safe-state and propose Security Integrity monitoring as a possible approach to address this issue. Bosch, Delphi, and Ford suggested a multi-level monitoring approach that redundantly calculates safety-critical paths for critical problem detection and fail-safe activation.

NHTSA Response: The agency is currently collecting some diagnostic and failure data from restraint and crash avoidance systems in some of its databases (EDRs and in EWR). As outlined in the FR notice, the agency has an ongoing interest in researching extended data logging needs as well as trigger points for purposes of evidence capture during electronic system failures. Further, NHTSA is researching a typology to better serve the purpose of detecting electronic control system failure indications in some of its databases.

NHTSA will continue to monitor and provide guidance to industry practices and activities in advanced prognostics, diagnostics, integrated vehicle health monitoring and management. As research continues, the agency will be in a better position to determine whether there is a need for additional involvement in this area.

NHTSA concurs that the safety ramifications of different types of potential security breaches into an automotive control system may vary significantly in severity. The agency is closely following the industry initiatives through standards-setting bodies in order to establish automotive security integrity levels analogous to the ASILs defined within the ISO 26262 functional safety standard. The agency agrees that it may be prudent to consider cybersecurity threat pathways early in the design phases to mitigate the possibility of a cybersecurity breach to result in the potential violation of a safety goal for an item associated with a high safety integrity level requirement, particularly for safety-critical systems that govern the motion controls of a vehicle.

The agency is interested in continuing to research whether it is possible and practical to design automotive electronic control systems in a manner that, even in situations when all security measures may be by-passed, integrity and robustness of key safety-critical control functions (e.g., throttle, brake, steering, and motive power) can still be sustained.

6. RFC Response Summary for Standards Conformity and Process Certification

Continental, Ford, Schaeffler, SAE International and TRW noted that ISO 26262 includes both conformation and verification requirements. Moreover, similar well-trusted measures have been successfully applied in other industries for the same purpose (e.g., electrotechnical industry and medical products). Still, it was conversely noted that conformity should not be regulated. Alliance, Ford, Global and Mercedes-Benz, however, suggested that NHTSA should collaborate with industry in forums such as CAMP and standards-setting organizations to develop and evaluate approaches for manufacturers to demonstrate conformity to an industry standard. ASC, Global, GM, MEMA and SAE International cautioned the agency that certification to a specific guideline and pass/fail criteria could have the potential to become prescriptive and take development focus away from other existing methods and practices. They recommended that NHTSA should avoid implementing a certification process for system engineering or recommending any generic performance tests, due to the variation among products and the difficulty in normalizing results. Related to certification, Continental stated that "process certifications" such ISO 15504 (SPICE) or CMMI bases are not suitable to support or improve safety development. They indicated that, generally speaking, "process certifications" based on process capability models neither address the applied methods nor the design itself; when it comes to evaluation of the suitability and effectiveness of development methods and their results, the specific area of application needs to be considered (e.g., the functions and properties of the specific component developed.) With respect to safety, Continental stated that generic third-party certification approach would not provide a benefit, especially when the approach may not be able to adequately reflect the specific area of application of a control system. Conversely, Antony Anderson stated that NHTSA should consider implementing a third-party safety certification. William Scherlis of Carnegie-Mellon University noted that process compliance is only indirectly associated with quality outcomes.

NHTSA Response: NHTSA acknowledges the cautionary comments from the manufacturers suggesting that potential conformance/certification requirements for process standards are not only difficult to set, but also may have unintended consequences. NHTSA is cognizant of the challenges in developing and enforcing requirements for process standards and will continue to research their feasibility through collaboration and stakeholder engagement.

V.2. Security Needs to Prevent Unauthorized Access to Electronic Components

Cybersecurity recommendations were made to the following three areas:

1. Technical areas for further research
2. Security process standards
3. Security performance tests

1. RFC Response Summary for Technical Areas for Further Research

The RFC respondents consistently agreed that no real-world vehicular cyber-attack has actually occurred, however, they also concurred that it is a possibility. Almost all responses indicated that a remote cyberattack is a greater threat than a local cyberattack. However, Andre Weimerskirch of University of Michigan Transportation Research Institute made the point that all potential attack surfaces should be equal in importance. Micron stated that physical access to hardware exposes more attack surface than remote access.

More generally, Bosch and Delphi proposed a “layered” approach to security in which vehicle ECUs are isolated from each other by switches and firewalls. The respondents also identified several problematic technical features:

- The lack of CAN bus source validation (Delphi);
- Unsecured debugging and diagnostic interfaces (Bosch);
- GM and Computer Emergency Response Team (CERT) at Carnegie-Mellon are both concerned about consumer devices which plug into the OBD-II port; and
- CERT and Donald Slavik both recommend that wireless systems should be completely isolated from the CAN bus.

The responses to technical questions did reveal some differences in recommended approach. For instance, CERT and Bosch stated that remote programming and diagnostics of safety-critical control units introduce new vulnerabilities, while GM states that over-the-air (remote) updates can remediate vulnerabilities. When asked about prominent hacking techniques, Bosch cited the misuse of debugging interfaces. In contrast, TRW cited the misuse of user interfaces.

There were several other comments which deserve mention:

- Ford commented that intrusion detection is an area which deserves attention;
- TRW commented that a compromised cellular base station could cause potential challenges;
- Digante Das with CALCE at University of Maryland strongly emphasized a need for a Counterfeit Electronics Control Plan, such as the adoption of the suite of SAE International standards[48] from the aviation, aerospace and defense industries aimed to stop counterfeit electronics parts from entering the supply chain, inventory and design; and

- Micron made the point that any non-volatile memory hardware which does not have cryptographic protection is vulnerable to code exfiltration and modification

NHTSA Response: NHTSA will continue to research system security assessment processes and techniques used in automotive and other related industries. The feedback on the use of a layered approach to security is in line with the viewpoint that NHTSA outlined in the FR notice. More research in this area is needed to assess the risks and potential mitigation effects of various alternatives, such as over-the-air (OTA) software updates. However, as the agency outlined in the FR notice, overall system resiliency against cyber threats can be improved by viewing system architectures in terms of "layers" or zones of protection.

NHTSA acknowledges that there could be potential cybersecurity concerns associated with aftermarket replacement parts, which may also be subject to counterfeit risks. The agency will examine the suggested suite of voluntary standards from the aviation, aerospace and defense industries for their applicability to motor vehicles.

NHTSA concurs that remote attack threats are of high interest; however, it also agrees that aftermarket products, such as a device with remote wireless capabilities plugged into the onboard diagnostics port, could convert a local cyber threat (such as a threat requiring physical access inside the vehicle) into a remote wireless threat. Hence, the threat assessment process must take reasonable use case scenarios into account and boundaries for minimal requirements may not be trivial to establish by only considering system capabilities at the time of a vehicle's build.

2. RFC Response Summary for Security Process Standards

ISO 26262 seems to have acquired some acceptance as a safety process standard. However, the use of ISO 26262 to provide a framework for cybersecurity does not appear to be globally agreeable. Although MEMA suggested "Integrating Safety and Security is Key," the responses regarding security process standards universally suggest that security does not fit into a general safety process. Bosch specifically mentioned that ISO26262 cannot be used as a security process standard. Bosch, Delphi, GM, SAE International and TRW indicated that several standards are available (or nearly available) that could address electronic component and security concerns not addressed by voluntary safety process standards, including updated ISO 26262, Internet Engineering Task Force (IETF) RFC 2196, International Society for

Automation (ISA)/IEC 62443, NIST's Federal Information Processing Standard (FIPS), and Payment Card Industry (PCI) security standards. However, Alliance, Global, and Information Technology Industry Council did not support establishing security process standards. In fact, Alliance in particular suggested that security process standards could actually create security vulnerabilities. Generally, cybersecurity is seen as a dynamic complex problem which may not be effectively addressed with the use of a static standard. On the other hand Bosch and MEMA pointed out that safety and cybersecurity convergence may be needed due to their relationship in vehicle-level hazards.

NHTSA Response: The agency agrees that ISO 26262 deals with random failures related to automotive electrical and electronic systems and does not necessarily address cybersecurity. Based on its review of process standards summarized in this report, the agency believes that there is a role for robust standards to assess cybersecurity risks, associated safety hazards, and mitigation priorities for automotive electronics. However, NHTSA acknowledges the differences in opinion among public responses on this topic, and the agency believes that more research is needed to assess the value and practicability associated with potential broader security process standardization or setting minimum set of baseline security measures. The agency's research on electronic systems safety and security also suggests that "design for safety" and "design for security" concepts as well as requirements driven from contemporary functional safety approaches and emerging security methods may have overlapping domains. There may be benefits to harmonizing these requirements particularly for safety-critical functions.

NHTSA will explore additional security process standards to the extent they are applicable or adaptable to a cyber-physical system such as an automobile. NHTSA's general approach is to set design-independent minimum standards that are facts-based and can be objectively tested. Security processes and standards as well as safety processes and standards continue to interest the agency from the standpoint of benefits, challenges and overall safety impacts. The agency will continue its research in collaboration with stakeholders to determine policy alternatives for the agency to consider.

3. RFC Response Summary for Security Performance Tests

In general, the respondents agreed that they were not aware of security performance standard metrics. On the other hand, they also agreed that metrics and procedures are needed to test the resilience of vehicle systems against cyber-attacks under various research-based and real-world scenarios. TRW stated that traditional IT security metrics could be useful. Ford mentioned traditional IT security metrics as well, but suggested that they may not be applicable in the context of automobile cybersecurity.

When the RFC respondents were asked to provide specific design characteristics which can help ensure a minimum level of security, both Bosch and Denso discussed secure diagnostic access to ECUs. Denso stated "for ECU firmware protection: limiting or prohibiting access to the debugging port." Bosch, Delphi and TRW discussed authentication and non-repudiation approaches.

Several respondents stated that there are no standard security assurance tools or tests. Mercedes-Benz stated that it has security assurance tools, but the tools are proprietary.

SAE International made the point that publishing standard security tests is not a good idea since the tests themselves may be exploited as vulnerabilities.

NHTSA Response: NHTSA's general approach is to set design-independent minimum standards that are facts-based and can be objectively tested. To the extent possible, the agency will explore performance metrics and tests that are design- and OEM- independent. However, the agency acknowledges the public's view on the difficulty associated with this objective considering the large number of electrical architecture and implementation variations that exist across manufacturers, vehicle models and even model years. Further, because of the dynamically-changing nature of cybersecurity threats and adversary capabilities, any set standards may become quickly outdated. NHTSA is also considering several alternatives including developing cybersecurity guidelines, principles or best practices.

V.3. Effects of Surrounding Environment on Electronic Component Performance

The respondents agreed that NHTSA has considered primary ways the environment can impact electronic system performance. Recommendations about the impact of the environment were made in two areas: EMC/EMI and research topics concerning sensors and the environment:

1. RFC Response Summary for EMC and EMI Susceptibility

The RFC responses fall into three major categories.

a. NHTSA should encourage voluntary EMC standards/performance metrics for aftermarket products that ensure compatibility with today's automotive electrical/electronic systems.

The agency should lead collaborative effort with OEMs and aftermarket electronic device suppliers to adopt existing industry standards and performance requirements for all involved parties. (Ford, GM, SAE International)

b. NHTSA should allow auto manufacturers to continue to define/ensure appropriate EMC/EMI tests. NHTSA should not regulate a methodology since it can impose constraints and negatively impact innovation. (ASC)

c. NHTSA should not engage in this overall area of research as needs are already met (Mercedes-Benz). The current state-of-the-art in EMC/EMI design and testing standards is suggested to be sufficient. Delphi stated that NHTSA should be in contact with the automotive EMC community, SAE, ISO, International Special Committee on Radio Interference, etc.. Delphi further stated that actively knowing/participating in standards work will ensure NHTSA and others are in tune with the present state of the art. Delphi also stated that as NHTSA may not have resources to actively participate in all committees, at a minimum NHTSA can request regular updates from the major committees (as some other government agencies do.) Delphi believed that, through active participation, it will become evident to NHTSA that there is a robust set of requirements that exceed regulatory requirements both nationally and internationally.

NHTSA Response: The agency acknowledges the comment that aftermarket products, such as consumer devices or peripherals that may be brought on board the vehicle, could influence the EMI levels experienced by automotive electronics. At this time, NHTSA believes that collaborative industry effort through SAE International's Electromagnetic Compatibility (EMC) Standards Committee may be the best venue for manufacturers and suppliers to assess the safety risks, and potential mitigation approaches and alternatives. NHTSA will monitor the ongoing research and discussions on this topic and assess whether there is benefit for the agency to be involved at another level. NHTSA understands that there is broad support for the existing model for EMC/EMI and that comments did not support an explicit need for the agency to be more involved in this area.

2. RFC Response Summary for Research Topics about Sensors and the Environment

The RFC responses fall into three main categories.

a. NHTSA should research the environmental impact on the following sensor technologies:

- Magnetic sensor integrated circuits, which are extremely susceptible when exposed to field-coupled electrostatic discharge. (Bosch)
- Sensors with low-level signals (Delphi and GM) and high-gain stages.
- Non-contacting sensors. (Ford, GM, and SAE International)

b. NHTSA should examine the constantly-changing external radio frequency (RF) environment present to road vehicles and work with public, private, and military sources to ensure that exposure levels are consistent with those used by automotive OEMs.

c. NHTSA may wish to consider that the surrounding environment encompasses not just electromagnetic interference, but also includes other ways that the environment can impact the vehicle electronics (temperature, dust, fluid, immersion, vibration, mechanical shock, etc.) (Delphi and ASC)

NHTSA Response: The agency will use public recommendations to assess whether these types of sensing technologies need to be researched further for susceptibility to environmental effects or whether their potential vulnerabilities would be captured and accounted for by the "design for functional safety" approach at the vehicle level. NHTSA also acknowledges the public recommendation for the agency to look into the potential electromagnetic radiation related health hazards that may arise from the fast growing use of automotive sensors.

NHTSA believes that three primary ways outlined in the FR notice related to how the environment can affect electronic components, namely, by potentially causing (1) electronic components to fail prematurely; (2) electronic control systems to act in unintended ways; and (3) electronic sensors or systems to perceive the environment differently than reality, and the subsequent discussion in that section already acknowledges the environment's effects beyond just EMC/EMI.

V.4. General Topics Related to Electronic System Safety and Cybersecurity

This is a summary of responses that generally and specifically fall under the RFC's "Additional Comments Requested" section. Respondents made recommendations in three areas:

1. RFC Response Summary for Additional Data Sources for Identification of Trends

American Automobile Association wanted better NHTSA database interfaces for 3rd party data aggregators. Bosch suggested that the agency consider international databases. IIHS suggested that NHTSA should consider establishing a unified data log of system and subsystem failures. Upon any servicing, a technician would upload the vehicle's system failure data into the unified data log. If designed properly, NHTSA could use the log to quickly identify the source and frequency of failures, even if a system corrected itself and the driver was unaware. TRW stated that the current relevant sources of retrospective data appear complete. TRW further recommended that NHTSA pursue research for data relevant to future systems that takes into account historical data, technology roadmaps supporting the NHTSA Preliminary Statement of Policy Concerning Automated Vehicles, and a predictive model to produce data for use by the automotive industry.

NHTSA response: The agency will consider public comments in its pursuit to investigate other data sources that may be relevant to the agency's determination of priority areas for electronics and cybersecurity research. Some of the public recommendations in this area refer to establishing new databases, which is also an area of research pursued by the agency.

2. RFC Response Summary for Traceability Improvement

RFC respondents suggested that, given the ephemeral nature of software and cyber-physical system failures, it is important to trace software events as they occur. Several individuals (Anderson, Armstrong, Gaasbeck and Hensler), along with a couple of industry associations (IIHS and ASC), expressed a strong desire for better data logging capabilities beyond the capabilities of EDRs. Expert witnesses and trial lawyers saw more capable data logging technologies as a necessary public window into the functioning of light vehicles, while these industry associations see them as a necessary debugging tool for increasingly complex systems. Delphi added that SAE J1698[49] recommended practice provides guidelines for standardization of recording certain malfunction information and could possibly serve as a framework for recording additional malfunction or traceability data in data loggers. Advocates for Highway and Auto Safety commented that the agency does not mention the need for improvement of the regulation for EDRs to ensure that they capture pertinent data relevant to electronic systems.

NHTSA response: The agency agrees that traceability of electronics and software related issues and cybersecurity concerns heavily depend upon the availability of robust data. Without a record-of-data from the vehicle and the electronic systems and/or components, it could prove difficult to differentiate between the sources of a potential vehicle level issue (e.g. driver misuse, electronics malfunction or a cyber-attack). There are good examples from the recent past regarding how vehicle data has been used to serve NHTSA's investigative processes. For instance, EDR data was used to better understand pedal misapplication in the Toyota unintended and uncontrolled acceleration investigation.[50] In addition, EDR data was also used in determining the ignition switch position in the General Motors ignition switch recall campaign[51]. However, as mentioned in Section III of this report, EDR data may have limitations to serve a similar role in some other cases. Considering the large number of ECUs and high volume communications that take place on a vehicular network, it is still an open area of research to identify effective strategies to define necessary and sufficient datasets as well as appropriate trigger logic for logging such data. The needs associated with cases with an internally-detected electronic failure differ from cases where there are no detected failures. The overarching intent is to improve traceability of potential concerns for both cases and the latter set of scenarios poses bigger challenges. However, it is clear that data logging has a significant role in improving the traceability of electronics and cybersecurity concerns. The agency plans to initiate new research into this topic pending availability of resources.

3. RFC Response Summary for Other General Comments

- Geoffrey Barrance stated that the RFI (RFC) cannot be responded to in the terms that it requests. He further stated that it has a fundamental error of perspective and scope. In addition, he expressed the thought that NHTSA needs professional Systems Engineers, qualified to assess vehicle and electronic system designs, and with experience of Hazard Analysis, FMEA, down to the system architecture, hardware, and software implementation levels. Furthermore, Mr. Barrance states that NHTSA should make a study of FAA and National

Transportation Safety Board (NTSB) practices, suggesting that the agency model itself after the FAA and NTSB.

- Gerard Holzmann stated that the RFC contains no mention of software safety, or software standards, as a primary consideration; and that the key issues related to software use in passenger vehicles are perhaps not being recognized as a driving concern affecting the safety and security of current and future passenger vehicles. Mr. Holzmann suggested that NHTSA emphasize software standards in this domain, and a focused examination of the process that should be followed by vendors to demonstrate the compliance of their products with these standards and assess whether it has sufficient expertise in software safety and software security to perform this examination, and if not how it could obtain this expertise.
- Advocates for Highway and Auto Safety cautioned the agency to not lose focus on the need for safety standards to address electronics in current safety systems by instead preparing only for the problems to be addressed to achieve full vehicle automation. Significant strides can and should be taken to ensure the safety of electronics in current systems which can and likely will develop into the standards required to ensure the success of automated vehicles and the predicted resultant safety benefits.
- SAE International stated that RFC did not ask specific questions with respect to human factors. SAE International further stated that since the proliferation of vehicle sensors and active safety technologies will become more prevalent to achieve automated vehicles, there is a definite future need, as well as 'identified and funded research' by NHTSA, to logically review and determine any potential 'safety and human factors' impact to the driver and vehicle occupants with respect to cybersecurity.
- MEMA requested that NHTSA release its new "Research and Rulemaking Priority Plan." It stated that, documents like the priority plan are very useful to the public and industry stakeholders as they plan for the future and anticipate potential changes to standards and opportunities for technology research.
- Stephen Van Gaasbeck suggested that NHTSA should promulgate rules which prohibit the transmission of vehicle data to the manufacturer without the consent of the vehicle owner. IEEE suggested that NHTSA's safety culture does not allow for adequate

prioritization of privacy or consumer protection issues with respect to safety.

- Delphi reiterated that the electronic control systems being discussed for evaluation enable dramatic improvements in passenger safety through, among other improvements to vehicle safety, the implementation of active safety technologies.

NHTSA response: NHTSA acknowledges the comments from the public suggesting NHTSA adopt an oversight role similar to, for instance, the FAA. The agency has studied other regulatory agency approaches, including the FAA's. However, there are significant practical and authority challenges. NHTSA's authority is significantly different than FAA's authority. The Safety Act[52] establishes a self-certification framework for ensuring compliance with the safety standards. Under this framework, NHTSA establishes performance standards for motor vehicles and motor vehicle equipment to which manufacturers of these products are required to certify that their products conform. NHTSA does not certify or approve products. NHTSA also has concerns about the practical nature of establishing the capabilities to perform code and architecture reviews for every variant of vehicles produced in a timely and productive manner. Further, NHTSA is not aware of data suggesting that a type-approval system would yield different safety results than the existing self-certification process for electronic control systems.

The agency does consider software safety as an important aspect of electronic control system design and investigates available standards and best practices in this domain as a stand-alone topic as well as part of the ISO-26262 process (Part 6 of the standard). However, the detailed code-examination concept faces similar practicality- and authority-related challenges outlined above.

The programs outlined in the FR notice and in this report focus on current generation automotive electronics. The agency concurs that any requirements, guidelines, principles, or best practices developed for these systems will likely provide a foundation for more advanced forms of automated vehicles.

While human factors considerations are not the core focus of this examination, NHTSA recognizes the importance and relevance of human factors to traffic safety across the full spectrum of vehicle automation levels (which includes lower levels of automation, which are also referred as crash avoidance functions).

NHTSA published its latest research priority plan[53] in June 2015.

The agency acknowledges that increased traceability of electronics-related anomalies through expanded data logging and transmission could have privacy implications and need to be considered in the process. It also agrees that electronics do bring in immense benefits in terms of safety, efficiency, and convenience; and that any actions that may be taken toward improving cybersecurity of vehicles should try not to adversely impact safety benefits that are attained through these advanced technologies.

VI. Conclusion

VI.1. Highest Priority Vehicle Systems for Safety

The agency considers that the highest priority vehicle components with respect to automotive electronic control systems include the propulsion, braking, steering, and motive power control systems, which directly influence the fundamental dynamic motion controls of a vehicle. NHTSA has been pursuing hazard analyses and safety requirements research in these priority safety-critical areas that received an overwhelming support from public response to the RFC (Table 2 in Appendix B). Even in the cases indicated with disagreement, the respondents requested other systems to be included in the priority list in addition to the proposed systems. NHTSA will move onto the analysis of other safety-relevant systems as resources permit; e.g., restraints systems, ADAS, etc. Expanding the research beyond motion control systems to include other automotive electronic control systems will further inform the agency about the operational capabilities, limitations, and associated hazards of safety-relevant vehicle control systems. The public also agrees that traditional databases NHTSA considered have limitations for use in identifying and revising priority areas from electronics and cybersecurity concerns stand-points and that additional sources, strategies or methods need research (Table 5 in Appendix B). Pending availability of resources, NHTSA plans to establish new research into exploring data elements and data recording trigger points for capturing record-of-data in cases of suspected electronics malfunctions and cybersecurity hacking attempts and will consider public comments submitted to RFC in developing the associated research plans.

VI.2. Potential Need for New Safety Standards

NHTSA has historically issued performance standards at the vehicle level. The standards contain specific test scenarios based on well-established criteria. By using scenarios that replicate real-world conditions, they seek to ensure that vehicles that perform well in the tests will also perform well in the real-world. This approach is taken both with regard to structural integrity and to the capabilities of an automotive system (e.g., Electronic Stability Control (ESC), which has electrical, electronic, mechanical and software elements).

While our existing rulemaking and investigative processes already cover electronic systems through the use of performance metrics and standards, we are investigating approaches to effectively address the safety assurance challenges associated with the increasingly-complex multitude of safety-critical electronic systems used in modern vehicles in relation to the multitude and variety of scenarios in which they are expected to perform but could fail. Implementing standards that provide for testing vehicles in all of those scenarios could be cost and time prohibitive. As such, our research is also evaluating any need for process standards. Specifically, the agency is seeking clarification of its authority to prescribe standards for motor vehicle functional safety process in the GROW AMERICA Act[54] proposal.

Success in identifying, analyzing and responding to potential automotive electronics concerns, including those related to cybersecurity issues, relies on the availability of robust data. These types of data from underlying electronic systems are typically not part of traditional crash databases. EDR type data, which can record detailed vehicle, electronic system and sensor data potentially before, during and following a driver perceived or experienced anomalous vehicle behavior has the potential to enhance the traceability of the potential issues. With suitably rich data, differentiating between various potential sources of root cause (e.g. driver issue, vehicle issue, cybersecurity issue) could become systematically possible. First, we plan to explore the range of data that is already being collected by and stored on the multitude of ECUs that enable crash avoidance and other advanced functions on vehicles today, and how that data could be shared with and used by NHTSA. Further, pending availability of resources, NHTSA plans to establish new research into exploring data elements and data recording trigger points for capturing record-of-data in cases of suspected electronics malfunctions and cybersecurity hacking attempts and will consider public comments submitted to RFC in developing the associated research plans.

Consistent with the NAS recommendation for the agency "to become more familiar with and engaged in standard-setting and other industry efforts that are aimed at strengthening the means by which manufacturers ensure the safe performance of their automotive electronics systems," as well as public feedback received on this topic, the agency intends to continue its involvement in the evolution of industry process standards for the safe development of automotive electronic control systems.

VI.2.1. Electronics Components and the Interaction of Electronic Components

The agency will pursue research to identify safety requirements needed for safety-critical control systems that govern vehicle motion. This research uses an analytical process based on parts of the ISO 26262 process standard that is being widely used across the industry to provide a good framework to manage the complexities associated with electrical/electronic control system failures. Through this series of research projects, the agency is gaining applied insights on the utility and limitations of the ISO 26262 standard in addition to developing functional safety requirements for key motion control systems. The agency has already positioned itself as an active participant in standards setting organization committees and will work with them and the OEMs to incorporate agency findings and input into new revisions.

The ISO 26262 process is being voluntarily adopted by the industry by virtue of being the stateof-art standard in the field of electronic systems development for automotive applications. The process establishes uniform and consistent boundary interfaces between OEMs and suppliers, which improves communications between parties related to requirements and expectations. Further, the standard requires extensive documentation and provision for traceability of design actions to underlying requirements. These attributes serve to improve transparency of the development process. However, as many of the public's comments also pointed out, there is no provision for certification of compliance with the ISO 26262 standard.

Alternatives for a potential government role in the area of robust industry process standards for functional safety are still being researched. The agency is already actively engaging in researching the strengths and gaps of the voluntary standards and providing input to the standard setting organizations. Other potential NHTSA involvement alternatives, as well as needs, benefits, potential enforcement of such involvement require further research. Based on 1) the agency's detailed one-on-one discussions with OEMs and major suppliers related to functional safety, 2) our engagement with the industry standards setting groups and participation in industry conferences and events related to ISO 26262, and 3) the public comments received in response to NHTSA's electronics RFC, we believe that the passenger vehicle industry is taking steps to adopt and update the ISO 26262 standard.

VI.2.2. Security Needs to Prevent Unauthorized Access to Electronic Components

In the area of cybersecurity, both our research and public comments indicate that there are no widely used automotive industry standards at this time, even though various organizations have developed their own internal processes and SAE International is investigating the possibility of establishing a cybersecurity standard analogous to ISO 26262. Some commenters also indicate that establishing uniform standards for automotive cybersecurity could adversely impact the cybersecurity posture for motor vehicles. NHTSA believes that commenters use the term "cybersecurity" interchangeably in the context of standards to mean "security" as well as "risk assessment and mitigation." The agency believes that there is a role for robust standards to assess cybersecurity risks, associated safety hazards, and mitigation priorities for automotive electronics. However, NHTSA acknowledges the differences in opinion among public responses related to standardizing security measures, and the agency believes that more research is needed to assess the value and practicability associated with potential standardization of a minimum set of baseline security measures.

Protection of automotive systems against cybersecurity risks could take various forms based on the underlying electrical/electronic network architecture used by manufacturers. A layered approach is often cited as offering the best form of protection. On the other hand, even though the layers of security progressively lower the probability of a security breach, they may not be able to eliminate the possibility of a successful cyber-attack altogether. Therefore, it may be prudent for cybersecurity to be considered upfront in the development process in conjunction with functional safety; i.e., a robust design based on a comprehensive functional safety process may need to be able to place the safety-critical systems of the vehicle in a safe state even if there were no security measures in place (i.e., if all layers of security are by-passed).

Due to the highly-dynamic nature of cybersecurity risks and threats, performance standards are difficult to set without the risk of becoming outdated quickly. Comments submitted in response to our FR notice also strongly advice against the agency's pursuing standards on cybersecurity for the same reason. Instead, developing cybersecurity guidelines could be more practical in this area. This approach is very common across various other industries and among federal agencies with regulatory authority, such as FDA and FAA. The agency is actively conducting research that could support the potential development of guidelines for the cybersecurity of automotive electronics.

Further, NHTSA also advocates that the industry proactively establish and be part of an information sharing forum such as an automotive ISAC. Sharing of timely information over signatures of potential cybersecurity concerns with the rest of the industry would provide for an effective response mechanism that has been proven to work in other industries. Related to this activity, in July 2015, Alliance and Global announced that they have completed the specifications for the ISAC needed for the automotive sector and that the industry will be voluntarily developing and launching an Auto ISAC with an expected start of operations by yearend 2015. In conjunction, NHTSA has been working closely with various federal agencies with overlapping interests in the vehicle domain, particularly in the area of cybersecurity, to facilitate open exchange of intelligence pertaining to potential cybersecurity solutions and research, as well as potential and future threats. For example, on the research side, NHTSA is coordinating closely with Defense Advanced Research Projects Agency (DARPA) on researching the cybersecurity of Vehicle-to-Vehicle communication interfaces, DHS's Homeland Security Advanced Research Projects Agency, NIST's National Cybersecurity Center of Excellence, and National Science Foundation's (NSF) Cyber-Physical Systems program directorate on their ongoing and future research investments in the automotive cybersecurity research domain. On the threats side, NHTSA is linked into DHS's Homeland Security Information Network - Critical Infrastructures (HSIN-CI) and National Infrastructure Coordination Center (NICC) partnership distribution group to benefit from future threat and intelligence information. Information and intelligence sharing is similarly essential (as improving traceability of in-vehicle electronics) to effectively respond to potential future real-world concerns.

A particular cybersecurity research topic area which NHTSA would like to explore with high priority is the cybersecurity of firmware[55] updates for automotive electronics. NHTSA's research interest from the standpoint of cybersecurity considerations covers both OTA updates and direct updates through physical interfaces. The OTA updates, in particular, are frequently cited as offering the means to expeditiously disseminate patches for newly-identified cybersecurity vulnerabilities as well as to potentially remedy recalls associated with software issues. However, OTA firmware updates need further research to ensure that they can be performed securely and safely and that capabilities which facilitate remote updates do not introduce critical threats and associated safety concerns.

VI.2.3. Effects of the Surrounding Environment on Electronic Component Performance

In the area of potential safety requirements related to environmental effects of automotive electronic systems and sensors, the agency currently does not find a need to pursue regulations or near-term research beyond the voluntary standards the industry already uses. Public comments also concur with the agency's position (Appendix B, Table 4). However, we agree with the public feedback on continuing to monitor and research the EMI effects on low-power signal and non-contact sensing technologies pending availability of agency resources.

VII. SUMMARY

This report fulfills the requirement of MAP-21, Division C, Title I, Subtitle D, Section 31402, Subsection (a), which required NHTSA to report to Congress on its examination of the need for safety standards and the highest priority areas for safety with regard to electronic systems in passenger motor vehicles. This examination considered the electronic components, the interaction of electronic components, the security needs for those electronic systems to prevent unauthorized access, and the effect of surrounding environments on the electronic systems. Moreover, MAP-21directed the agency to solicit public comments on its findings of this examination and to include public response in the report.

On October 7, 2014, NHTSA issued the RFC on the safety and security of automotive electronic control systems. As part of this RFC, NHTSA first outlined its strategic research program highlighting current agency approaches on examining the need for safety standards concerning electronic systems in passenger motor vehicles. NHTSA then sought feedback from a variety of organizations including OEMs, industry associations, and automotive suppliers on its research perspective and application of safety standards and processes. A total of 40 organizations and individuals responded to the RFC.

This report analyzed the responses and summarized their key themes and recommendations.

Based on its own examination and public feedback, NHTSA outlined key near-term research needs to enhance the safety and security of automotive safety-critical electronic control systems. In addition, NHTSA identified the highest priority control systems for safety research. Based on the investigation outlined in this report, the agency does not find a clear need for immediate new regulations above and beyond NHTSA's existing rulemaking activities on advanced technologies; however, we expect the near-term research results to inform the agency on whether to issue new performance or process standards, guidelines, principles or best practices related to automotive electronic control systems safety and/or security. NHTSA's research programs on vehicle electronic systems safety and cybersecurity will contribute to important and meaningful improvements in detection, traceability, mitigation, and prevention of potential electronic control system concerns and malfunctions. As NHTSA moves forward, we will continue to keep the public informed and move expeditiously to turn research results into appropriate actions.

APPENDIX A: "REQUEST FOR COMMENT" QUESTIONS

Electronics Components and the Interaction of Electronic Components

1) NHTSA currently has research underway that is evaluating the hazards associated with electronic control systems that could impact a vehicle's steering, throttle, braking and motive power first because they can impact the fundamental control functions that a driver performs (such as providing lateral (via steering) and longitudinal (throttle, braking) control for the vehicle). This means, we would research safety hazards associated with other automotive electronic control systems (e.g. safety restraint systems control, power door lock control, lighting control) later. We seek comment on this approach from a need for standards research priority stand-point.

a) Should the agency pursue alternative approaches to categorize and prioritize potential electronic control system hazards and impacts to support new standards?

b) For hazard analysis research, the agency is currently pursuing HazOp and STPA. What other hazard analysis methods should the agency also consider and why?

c) What other automotive electronics should we consider in our research that could affect the electronics in the safety-critical systems we identified (steering, throttle, brakes, etc.)?

2) NHTSA currently has research underway that is evaluating system performance requirements for critical safety systems. We seek comment on automotive electronic component and system performance requirements for control systems that impact throttle, braking, steering, and motive power management:

a) What performance-based tests, methods, and processes are now available for safety assurance of these types of automotive electronic control systems?

b) What series of performance-based tests should the agency consider to ensure safe functionality of these types of automotive electronic control systems under all real-world conditions (e.g. nominal, expected, non-nominal, and failure conditions)?

c) Performance tests would ideally be applicable regardless of any specific design choices.

We surmise that electronic components may have a wider variety of manufacturer specific tuning and implementation variations. What types of challenges does this create for designing performance tests for electronic components? What methods are available for addressing those challenges?

3) NHTSA currently has research underway that is evaluating diagnostics and prognostics for critical safety systems. We seek comment on vehicle health monitoring, diagnostics, and prognostics capabilities and fault-tolerant design alternatives for automotive safety applications.

a) What methods are effective in identifying potential anomalous behavior associated with electronic components, systems, and communications reliably and quickly?

b) What strategies do current vehicles have for activating a "fail-safe" mode when critical problems are detected? What types of problems are classified as "critical" and how does the vehicle detect these problems?

c) What state-of-the-art detection and fail-safe response methods should the agency be aware of and further assess?

4) NHTSA currently has research underway that is evaluating various process standards and their applicability to critical safety systems. We seek comment on testing, validation, certification, and regulation alternatives for vehicle electronics to these process standards: a) What are the pros and cons of utilizing a process - certification method (e.g., ISO 26262) where the

manufacturer is asked to identify, categorize, and consider potential remedies for electronics safety problems?

i) What approaches should be considered for manufacturers to demonstrate conformity with voluntary industry process standards such as ISO 26262?

ii) How does one evaluate conformity to a process standard that uses an engineer's best judgment to identify, categorize, and consider potential remedies to electronics safety problems?

iii) What verification steps may be appropriate to ensure that potential standards are met?

Security Needs To Prevent Unauthorized Access to Electronic Components

1) We seek comment on any technical areas of automotive cybersecurity that the agency could focus on in its further research.

a) Specifically, are there particularly vulnerable or strong design architectures that the agency should further examine?

b) What additional types of techniques (either in real world occurrences or as a part of research) have persons used to gain unauthorized access to vehicle systems? What types of systems were such persons able to gain access to?

c) What is the public's view on the differences in cybersecurity risks associated with an intrusion that requires use of in-cab physical interfaces (e.g. OBD-II port) versus close-proximity wireless interfaces (e.g. Bluetooth) versus long-range wireless means (e.g. cellular/satellite links)?

2) We seek comment on security process standards.

a) What security process standard alternatives are available? How do these standards differ and are there standards that are more suitable for application to the automotive industry versus others?

b) Could security assurance be handled within a modified framework of existing safety process standards (such as FMEAs, FTAs, ISO 26262) or does "design for security" require its own process?

3) We seek comments on security performance standards. In contrast to the process standards (that establish methods for considering cybersecurity risks during product design), we use the term "performance standard" to mean standards that evaluate the cybersecurity performance (or resilience) of a system after production of the final product.

a) What types of metrics are available to test a vehicle's ability to withstand a cyber-attack?

b) Are there any common design characteristics that help ensure a minimum level of security from unauthorized access to a vehicle's electronic control systems?

c) What performance-based tests, methods, and processes are available for security assurance of automotive electronic control systems?

d) Are there hardware, software, watchdog algorithm, etc. requirements or criteria that would help differentiate algorithm designs that are more secure against cyber-attack?

Effects of the Surrounding Environment on Electronic Component Performance

1) NHTSA has reviewed the state-of-the art with respect to environmental conditions and vehicle electronics. What other ways can the environment impact electronic system performance other than the ways that we have considered, above?

2) NHTSA has done some testing on interference issues. We seek comment in the area of EMI/EMC.

a) What could the agency do to further assess the electromagnetic interference (EMI) susceptibility impacts of growing use of electronics on automotive system safety and assess the adequacy of existing voluntary standards?

b) Are there known EMI susceptibility differences in vehicles designed and sold in the U.S. versus in regions where EMC may be explicitly regulated?

3) We seek comment in the area of the environment's potential impact on advanced automotive sensors.

a) Are any particular sensing technologies more susceptible or less susceptible to such effects (including EMC and other environmental effects such as moisture, corrosion, etc.)?

Additional Comments Requested

In addition to the comments requested in regards to the specific topics discussed above, we are also seeking comment on other general issues relating to electronic component safety and cybersecurity.

1) One issue that we seek comment is the potential for voluntary safety process standards to help address challenges introduced by expanding use of electronics in automotive applications. In section II.d. above, we discuss the various design and quality control processes that the industry already uses to

assess the safety and cybersecurity of their electronic components (e.g., ISO 26262).

a) We seek public comment on the degree to which this type of safety process standard can provide an adequate level of protection from electronic component failures or potential cybersecurity breaches.

i) What voluntary industry standards are best able to address safety assurance of electronics control system design for motor vehicles?

ii) Specifically, what elements of the voluntary industry standards are best able to address electronics control systems and cybersecurity issues in motor vehicles?

iii) What other standards than those described in this document are relevant for the agency to consider?

b) What types of concerns with regard to electronic components safety and cybersecurity would not be addressed by voluntary safety process standards?

i) What other standards are available that could address this type of safety concern?

ii) What software development, validation and safety assurance methods and processes are suitable for safety critical automotive control systems?

c) Are existing process standards such as ISO 26262, IEC 60812, IEC 61025, etc., suitable to address electronic control system design challenges for more advanced forms of vehicle automation?

2) Another issue that we seek comment on is in regards to the available information and data sources for identifying and understanding the issues related to electronic component reliability and cybersecurity. We recognize that much of the data available to the agency captures retrospective data. Thus, the traditional sources of information available to the agency have various limitations in this rapidly-developing area of automotive technology. Information that shows historic data on electronic component issues may not necessarily give an accurate prediction of what future electronic component reliability and cybersecurity issues can be. We seek comment on the data sources that are identified for potential consideration in the categorization of priority focus areas for electronics reliability.

a) We are especially interested in identifying any potential data sources that could assist the agency in identifying potential emerging electronic component failures in vehicles in a timely manner.

b) Has the agency considered all the relevant data on this subject? What additional sources of information could the agency consider?

3) We seek comment on what other information sources or strategies are available that can enhance the ability to detect potential electronics system

related concerns in a timely fashion. What methods are available to improve traceability of potential electronic control system malfunctions?

APPENDIX B: HIGH LEVEL SUMMARY OF "REQUEST FOR COMMENTS" RESPONSES

Figure 1 illustrates the breakdown of the number of respondents by seven groups. Table 1 shows the numbers of questions addressed in each topic area by the respondents. Some industry association committees and OEMs jointly developed responses to some RFC questions where there had been ongoing collaboration between the organizations; thus, there is some limited overlap of responses. Examples of salient or prevalent observations, and the number of comments provided, are summarized for each of the topic areas in Tables 2 through 5.

Figure 1. Breakdown of Respondents by Groups.

Table 1. Total Responses by Topic Area from 40 Respondents

Topic Area	Total Responses	Total Possible Responses
I. Electronic Components (13 Questions)	127	520
II. Security Needs (9 Questions)	107	360
III. Effect of Surrounding Environment (4 questions)	29	160
IV. Additional Comments (11 Questions)	60	440
Four Topic Areas (37 Questions)	323	1,480

Table 2. Comments on Electronic Components

Key Observations	Total Responses
Agreed ISO 26262 as industry standard	10/18
Agreed but with caveats/additional approaches	7/18
Disagreed with pursuing ISO 26262	1/18
Agreed with NHTSA's research prioritization approach	10/12
Disagreed in the sense that it must include othersystems	2/12
Suggested additional systems to consider	7/12

Table 3. Comments on Security Needs

Key Observations	Total Responses
"Design for security" requires its own process	6/8
Alternative security process standards proposed	8/8
No real world examples of techniques to gain unauthorized access to vehicle control systems	5/5

Table 4. Comments on Effects of Surrounding Environment

Key Observations	Total Responses
No known EM I susceptibility difference between vehicles sold in US and abroad	5/6
Regional differences can exist	1/6
Develop voluntary EM C standards and performance metrics for aftermarket devices	3/3

Table 5. Additional Comments

Key Observations	Total Responses
Bel i eve that exist existing process standards suitable to address electronic control system chal l enges for more advanced automation	2/4
Do not bel i eve existi ng standards are suitable for highly automated system development	2/4
Agreed that traditional databases have limitations and N HTSA should consider other relevant data sources	9/10
Bel i eves, existing databases are sufficient	1/10
Bel i eve other information sources, strategies or methods are available to enhance ability to detect electronics concerns and/or trace malfunctions	13/14

End Notes

[1] Moving Ahead for Progress in the 21st Century Act, Public Law 112-141 (Jul. 6, 2012), § 31402.

[2] Id.

[3] Id.

[4] Id.

[5] http://www.regulations.gov/#!docketDetail;D=NHTSA-2014-0108.

[6] Not including electronics use for radio purposes.

[7] "This car runs on code," R.N. Charette, 2009, http://spectrum.ieee.org/transportation/systems/this-car-runs-on-code.

[8] http://www.nhtsa.gov/About+NHTSA/Press+Releases/NHTSA-sets-AEB-plans,-highlights-lives-saved-repoot.

[9] http://www.nhtsa.gov/staticfiles/rulemaking/pdf/Automated Vehicles Policy.pdf.

[10] The Safety Promise and Challenge of Automotive Electronics, insights from unintended acceleration, National Research Council of the National Academies, ISBN 978-0-309-22304-1, 2012, http://onlinepubs.trb.org/onlinepubs/sr/sr308.pdf.

[11] "Experimental Security Analysis of a Modern Automobile," K. Koscher et. al., IEEE Symposium on Security and Privacy, Oakland, CA, 2010.

[12] "Comprehensive Experimental Analyses of Automotive Attack Surfaces," S. Checkoway et.al, USENIX Security, 2011.

[13] "Adventures in Automotive Networks and Control Units," C. Miller, C. Valasek, DEF CON 21, Las Vegas, NV, 2013.

[14] "Remote Exploitation of an Unaltered Passenger Vehicle," C. Miller, C. Valasek, BlackHat USA 2015, Las Vegas, NV, 2015.

[15] IEC 60812 standard covers the process for conducting FMEA analysis.

[16] IEC 61025 standard covers the process for conducting FTA analysis.

[17] ISO/TS 16949:2002 covers particular requirements for the application of ISO 9001:2000 for automotive production and relevant service part organizations.

[18] International Organization for Standardization (ISO) standard for Road vehicles – Functional safety.

[19] Van Eikema Hommes, Q., "Review and Assessment of the ISO 26262 Draft Road Vehicle - Functional Safety," SAE Technical Paper 2012-01-0025, 2012, doi:10.4271/2012-01-0025.

[20] IEC 61508 is an international standard for functional safety of electrical/electronic/ programmable electronic safety-related systems. This standard considers all of the environments that could result in an unsafe situation for the subject product, including shock, vibration, temperature, and electromagnetic fields and their induced voltages and currents.

[21] DO-178C: Software considerations in airborne systems and equipment certification.

[22] Airworthiness of an aircraft refers to meeting established standards for safe flight.

[23] ISO 26262-6:2011-Road vehicles; Functional safety; Part 6: Product development at the software level.

[24] http://www-odi.nhtsa.dot.gov/owners/SearchSafetyIssues.

[25] http://www.nhtsa.gov/NASS.

[26] http://www.nhtsa.gov/FARS.

[27] http://www.nhtsa.gov/SCI

[28] In 2006, NHTSA published a final rule creating a regulation (49 CFR Part 563, Event Data Recorders (Part 563)) that specifies the minimum data set that should be collected if a manufacturer decides to voluntarily install an EDR in their vehicle, along with requirements for the range and accuracy of EDR data, as well as requirements for storage and retrieval. Part 563 applies to vehicles manufactured on or after September 1, 2012. In December 2012, NHTSA proposed a standard that would mandate EDRs on all vehicles required to have frontal air bags. (77 FR 74144). No final rule publication date has been established.

[29] Moving Ahead for Progress in the 21st Century Act, Pub. L. No. 112-141 (Jul. 6, 2012), § 31401(a).

[30] Office of Vehicle Crash Avoidance & Electronic Control Research technical publications are posted on the NHTSA website at http://www.nhtsa.gov/Research/Crash+Avoidance/ Office+of+Crash+Avoidance+Research+Technical+Publications.

[31] Establishing a failure typology refers to developing categories and data elements that can help the agency (and others) organize the types of failures relating to electronic control systems in vehicles. Establishing the typology is an important step in helping to create a structure to help analyze potential safety problems relating to electronics in vehicles.

[32] "Framework for Improving Critical Infrastructure Cybersecurity," Version 1.0, NIST, 2014. Accessible at http://www.nist.gov/cyberframework/upload/cybersecurity-framework-021214.pdf.

[33] EVITA is a project co-funded by the European Union that aims to design, verify, and prototype architecture for automotive on-board networks where security-relevant components are protected against tampering and sensitive data are protected against compromise (http://www.evita-project.org/).

[34] The study report "An assessment of the information sharing and analysis center (ISAC) model" can be accessed at the "Automotive Cybersecurity Topics and Publications" docket: NHTSA-2014-0071.

[35] Correspondence related to this initiative can be viewed in the "Automotive Cybersecurity Topics and Publications" docket: NHTSA-2014-0071.

[36] Id.

[37] Such as those investigated in the Defense Advanced Research Projects Agency's (DARPA) high-assurance cyber military systems (HACMS) project. http://www.darpa.mil/Our Work/I2O/Programs/HighAssurance Cyber Military Systems (HACMS).aspx.

[38] "Tracking & Hacking: Security & Privacy Gaps Put American Drivers at Risk." February 2015. http://www.markey.senate.gov/imo/media/doc/2015-02-06 MarkeyReportTracking Hacking CarSecurity%202.pdf.

[39] A crystalline, hair-like structure of tin that can form on a tin-finished surface. (taken from NAS Report)

[40] SAE J551, SAE J1113

[41] ISO 7637, ISO 10605, ISO 11451, ISO 11452

[42] "Technical Support to the National Highway Traffic Safety Administration (NHTSA) on the Reported Toyota Motor Corporation (TMC) Unintended Acceleration (UA) Investigation," 2011, NASA. Section 6.8 of this report discusses the EMC testing and the full report can be accessed at http://www.nhtsa.gov/staticfiles/nvs/pdf/NASAUA report.pdf.

[43] DSRC band: 5.850 – 5.925 GHz.

[44] As of March 25, 2015, there have been 44 comments submitted to the docket (NHTSA-2014-0108), all of which have been considered by NHTSA.

[45] On February 13, 2015, NHTSA held a government roundtable on "Cybersecurity of safety-critical systems," which was attended by 14 agencies representing cyber-physical system security interests across surface transportation, aviation, medical, energy, forensics and military perspectives. At this event, participating agencies updated each other on their cybersecurity research findings and future direction and then collectively reviewed and provided feedback on NHTSA's automotive cybersecurity program plan.

[46] http://standards.sae.org/wip/j3061/

[47] For example, Federal Drug Administration published "Guidance for Industry and Food and Drug Administration Staff" on "Content of Premarket Submissions for Management of Cybersecurity in Medical Devices," in October 2014. (http://www.fda.gov/downloads/medicaldevices/deviceregulationandguidance/guidancedocuments/ucm356190.pdf)

[48] SAE AS5553 Counterfeit Electronic Parts; Avoidance, Detection, Mitigation; SAE ASP6178 Counterfeit Electronic Parts; Tools for Risk Assessment of Distributors; SAE AS6081 Counterfeit Electronic Parts; Avoidance, Protocol, Distributors; SAE 6171 Test Methods Standard; Counterfeit Electronic Parts.

[49] SAE J1698, Vehicle Event Data Interface-Vehicular Data Extraction, http://standards.sae.org/j1698/2 200405/

[50] NHTSA Action Number: RQ10-003. Details of the investigation can be accessed at http://wwwodi.nhtsa.dot.gov/owners/SearchSafetyIssues.

[51] NHTSA Campaign Number: 14V047000. Details of the campaign can be accessed at http://wwwodi.nhtsa.dot.gov/owners/SearchSafetyIssues.

[52] 49 U.S.C. §§ 30101 et seq.

[53] Overview of NHTSA Priority Plan for Vehicle Safety and Fuel Economy, 2015 to 2017. http://www.nhtsa.gov/staticfiles/nvs/pdf/NVS priority-plan-June2015 final.pdf.

[54] Sec. 4105 Functional Safety Process. http://www.transportation.gov/sites/dot.gov/files/docs/DOT surface reauthFINAL.pdf.

[55] "Firmware" refers to the software code and data that reside on an embedded system, such as an automotive electronic control system, that implements dedicated functions and manage system resources (e.g. system input/outputs (I/O) to execute those functions. Firmware is held in non-volatile memory (computer/device memory that does not lose stored information when the system is not powered) of an electronic device and may be rarely and –in cases- never gets updated during the lifetime of the product (post initial download). Typical reasons for updating firmware may include bug-fixes or adding new features to the system.

In: Safety Standards of Automotive Electronic ... ISBN: 978-1-63485-908-0
Editor: Michael J. Holmes

Chapter 2

TRACKING & HACKING: SECURITY & PRIVACY GAPS PUT AMERICAN DRIVERS AT RISK*

Staff of U.S. Senator Edward J. Markey

EXECUTIVE SUMMARY

New technologies in cars have enabled valuable features that have the potential to improve driver safety and vehicle performance. Along with these benefits, vehicles are becoming more connected through electronic systems like navigation, infotainment, and safety monitoring tools.

The proliferation of these technologies raises concerns about the ability of hackers to gain access and control to the essential functions and features of those cars and for others to utilize information on drivers' habits for commercial purposes without the drivers' knowledge or consent.

To ensure that these new technologies are not endangering or encroaching on the privacy of Americans on the road, Senator Edward J. Markey (D-Mass.) sent letters to the major automobile manufacturers to learn how prevalent these technologies are, what is being done to secure them against hacking attacks, and how personal driving information is managed.[1]

This report discusses the responses to this letter from 16 major automobile manufacturers: BMW, Chrysler, Ford, General Motors, Honda, Hyundai,

---

* This is an edited, reformatted and augmented version of a report issued February 2015.

Jaguar Land Rover, Mazda, Mercedes-Benz, Mitsubishi, Nissan, Porsche, Subaru, Toyota, Volkswagen (with Audi), and Volvo. Letters were also sent to Aston Martin, Lamborghini, and Tesla, but those manufacturers did not respond.

The responses reveal the security and privacy practices of these companies and discuss the wide range of technology integration in new vehicles, data collection and management practices, and security measures to protect against malicious use of these technologies and data. The key findings from these responses are:

1. Nearly 100% of cars on the market include wireless technologies that could pose vulnerabilities to hacking or privacy intrusions.
2. Most automobile manufacturers were unaware of or unable to report on past hacking incidents.
3. Security measures to prevent remote access to vehicle electronics are inconsistent and haphazard across all automobile manufacturers, and many manufacturers did not seem to understand the questions posed by Senator Markey.
4. Only two automobile manufacturers were able to describe any capabilities to diagnose or meaningfully respond to an infiltration in real-time, and most say they rely on technologies that cannot be used for this purpose at all.
5. Automobile manufacturers collect large amounts of data on driving history and vehicle performance.
6. A majority of automakers offer technologies that collect and wirelessly transmit driving history data to data centers, including third-party data centers, and most do not describe effective means to secure the data.
7. Manufacturers use personal vehicle data in various ways, often vaguely to "improve the customer experience" and usually involving third parties, and retention policies – how long they store information about drivers – vary considerably among manufacturers.
8. Customers are often not explicitly made aware of data collection and, when they are, they often cannot opt out without disabling valuable features, such as navigation.

These findings reveal that there is a clear lack of appropriate security measures to protect drivers against hackers who may be able to take control of a vehicle or against those who may wish to collect and use personal driver information.

In response to the privacy concerns raised by Senator Markey and others, the two major coalitions of automobile manufacturers recently issued a voluntary set of privacy principles by which their members have agreed to abide. These principles send a meaningful message that automobile manufacturers are committed to protecting consumer privacy by ensuring transparency and choice, responsible use and security of data, and accountability. However, the impact of these principles depend in part on how the manufacturers interpret them, because (1) the specific ways that transparency will be achieved are unclear and may not be noticed by the consumer, e.g., text in the user manual, (2) the provisions regarding choice for the consumer only address data sharing and do not refer to data collection in the first place, and (3) the guidelines for data use, security, and accountability largely leave these matters to the discretion of the manufacturers.

The alarmingly inconsistent and incomplete state of industry security and privacy practices, along with the voluntary principles put forward by industry, raises a need for the National Highway Traffic Safety Administration (NHTSA), in consultation with the Federal Trade Commission (FTC) on privacy issues, to promulgate new standards that will protect the data, security and privacy of drivers in the modern age of increasingly connected vehicles. Such standards should:

- Ensure that vehicles with wireless access points and data-collecting features are protected against hacking events and security breaches;
- Validate security systems using penetration testing;
- Include measures to respond real-time to hacking events;
- Require that drivers are made explicitly aware of data collection, transmission, and use;
- Ensure that drivers are given the option to opt out of data collection and transfer of driver information to off-board storage;

Require removal of personally identifiable information prior to transmission, when possible and upon consumer request.

INTRODUCTION AND METHODOLOGY

Today's cars and light trucks contain more than 50 separate electronic control units (ECUs), connected through a controller area network (CAN) or other network (such as Local Interconnect Networks or Flexray). Vehicle functionality, safety, and privacy all depend on the functions of these small computers, as well as their ability to communicate with one another. They also have the ability to record vehicle data to analyze and improve performance. On-board navigation technologies as well as the ability to integrate mobile devices with vehicle-based technologies have also fundamentally altered the manner in which drivers and the vehicles themselves can communicate during the vehicles' operation.

This new technology has also resulted in an increased ability to gather driving information. Such information-gathering abilities can be used by automobile manufacturers to provide customized service and improve customer experiences, but in the wrong hands such information could also be used maliciously. In particular, wireless technologies create vulnerabilities to hacking attacks that could be used to invade a user's privacy or modify the operation of a vehicle. Two recent developments highlight potential threats to both automobile security and to consumer privacy.

In a 2013 study that was funded by the Defense Advanced Research Projects Agency (DARPA), two researchers demonstrated their ability to connect a laptop to two different vehicles' computer systems using a cable, send commands to different ECUs through the CAN, and thereby control the engine, brakes, steering and other critical vehicle components.[2] In their initial tests with a laptop and two MY2010 vehicles from different manufacturers, they were able to cause cars to suddenly accelerate, turn, kill the brakes, activate the horn, control the headlights, and modify the speedometer and gas gauge readings.[3] More recently in 2014, those same researchers looked into the hackability of 21 different vehicle models from 10 different manufacturers, pointing out different levels of security in each vehicle with respect to wireless entry points, control points, and the types of computers than could be compromised.[4]

Before the researchers went public with their 2013 findings, they shared the results with the manufacturers in the hopes that the companies would address the identified vulnerabilities. But in response to the public release of the study, both companies reportedly noted that the researchers directly, rather than wirelessly, accessed the vehicles' computer systems, and referred to the need to prevent remote hacking from a wireless device. What the companies failed to note is that the DARPA study built on prior research that demonstrated that one could remotely and wirelessly access a vehicle's CAN bus through Bluetooth connections, OnStar systems, malware in a synced Android smartphone, or a malicious file on a CD in the stereo.[5]

A second, related area of concern relates to the increasing use of navigation or other technologies that could be used to record the location or driving history of those using them. A number of new services have emerged that permit the collection of a wide range of user data, providing valuable information not just to improve vehicle performance, but also potentially for commercial and law enforcement purposes.[6] This concern was highlighted when it was revealed that Tesla Motors recorded data during a test drive of one of its vehicles by a reporter and used data related to the driver's location, energy usage, speed, temperature and other control settings to rebut the reporter's unfavorable review of his driving experience.[7] Car dealerships and navigation systems providers have also begun to use "remote disabling," which enable them to track and disable vehicles if drivers do not keep up with their payments[8] or if cars have been reported as stolen, which can raise safety concerns if the vehicles are disabled during an emergency or when the driver is left stranded in an unsafe location.

Furthermore, vehicle-to-vehicle (V2V) technologies are emerging as a viable tool for improving active safety through collision avoidance, and one of the main unknowns in their development is a robust communication security system.[9] As vehicles continue to become more integrated with wireless technology, there are more avenues through which a hacker could introduce malicious code, and more avenues through which a driver's basic right to privacy could be compromised. These threats demonstrate the need for robust vehicle security policies to ensure the safety and privacy of our nation's drivers.

In order to better understand the ability of automobile companies to protect the safety and privacy of drivers, letters were sent to 20 major automobile manufacturers with questions regarding technology, security precautions, and privacy policies. The questions posed were identical for each manufacturer. Responses were received from 16 manufacturers. Tesla Motors, Aston Martin, and Lamborghini, did not respond to the letters. Volkswagen and Audi responded with a single letter and are together treated in the findings as a single responding manufacturer. Some manufacturers (notably Hyundai and Toyota) provided detailed, question-by-question responses, while others (notably Mercedes-Benz and Porsche) wrote generic statements on their commitments to security and privacy that were non-responsive to the questions that were posed.

Recently, and as a result of the questions posed by Senator Markey, the automobile industry has acknowledged the deficiencies and inconsistences between manufacturers in existing practices for vehicle privacy protections by issuing its own set of voluntary privacy principles.[10] These voluntary principles were developed and supported by the Alliance of Automobile Manufacturers and the Association of Global Automakers, which combined represent 23 major automobile manufacturers, including all of the manufacturers that responded to Senator Markey with the exception of Audi. The adopted principles include (1) transparency, (2) choice, (3) respect for context, (4) data minimization, de-identification and retention, (5) data security, (6) integrity and access, and (7) accountability. The establishment of these principles, and the agreement to them by 19 manufacturers (including all of those that responded to Senator Markey's letter with the exception of Jaguar Land Rover), represent an important step forward by the automotive industry.

Through the voluntary principles, the automakers assure consumers that they will be informed when data collection occurs and given choices regarding whether their information can be used for marketing purposes, companies will not pass on any information to law enforcement without a warrant or court order, and "reasonable" security measures will be in place to protect data from falling into the wrong hands. However, the principles continue to raise a number of questions regarding how car manufacturers will effectively make their practices transparent to consumers and provide consumers with rights to prevent sensitive data collection in the first place, among other concerns.

The diversity of responses received by Senator Markey shows that each manufacturer is handling the introduction of new technology in very different ways, and for the most part these actions are insufficient to ensure security and privacy for vehicle consumers. Individual automaker responses will not be publicly released due to the proprietary and security-sensitive nature of some of the responses. The following sections summarize the major findings from the analysis of responses conducted by Senator Markey's staff.

FINDINGS

Finding #1: Nearly 100% of cars on the market include wireless technologies that could pose vulnerabilities to hacking or privacy intrusions.

Wireless technologies in vehicles are becoming more prevalent as manufacturers have found ways that they can be used to improve safety, performance, and the driver experience. However, wireless technologies also require wireless entry points (WEPs), or ways that vehicle electronics can be accessed remotely. In 2011 a group of researchers showed WEPs in automobiles pose vulnerabilities, and they were able to remotely hack into a vehicle and exploit these vulnerabilities, including engaging in location tracking and eavesdropping, and controlling different features including the locks and brakes.[11]

Of the 16 manufacturers that responded to the letter, 14 provided information on the percentage of model year (MY) 2013 vehicles and the projected percentage of MY 2014 vehicles that have WEPs. Of the 14, 11 indicated that 100% of their vehicles have WEPs, and some of these manufacturers cited the federal mandate for tire pressure monitoring systems (TPMS) as a major contributor. Of the 3 who did not indicate that all vehicles have WEPs, the reported percentages of vehicles without WEPs were low, ranging from 7% to 30% and either stagnant or decreasing from 2013 to 2014.

These responses show that nearly all vehicles on the road have at least one WEP, and many vehicles have several WEPs. These include but may not be limited to TPMS, Bluetooth, keyless entry, remote start, navigation, Wi-Fi, cellular/telematics, radio, and anti-theft systems and features.

Finding #2: Most automobile manufacturers were unaware of or unable to report on past hacking incidents.

Senator Markey asked each of the manufacturers to list and describe instances in which they have been made aware of wireless or non-wireless infiltration events in their vehicles. Of the 16 manufacturers who responded to the letter, Jaguar Land Rover, Porsche, and Volkswagen did not respond to the question in any way. Of the 13 companies who did address the issue, 12 stated that they had no knowledge of any reported infiltration events, and only 1 reported such instances. This company described the following in detail:

- An application was developed by a third party and released for Android devices that could integrate with a vehicle through the Bluetooth connection. A security analysis did not indicate any ability to introduce malicious code or steal data, but the manufacturer had the app removed from the Google Play store as a precautionary measure.
- Some individuals have attempted to reprogram the onboard computers of vehicles to increase engine horsepower or torque through the use of "performance chips." Some of these devices plug into the mandated

onboard diagnostic port or directly into the under-the-hood electronics system.

Finding #3: Security measures to prevent remote access to vehicle electronics are inconsistent and haphazard across all automobile manufacturers, and many manufacturers did not seem to understand the questions posed by Senator Markey.

Manufacturers were asked how they assess their security against WEP infiltration, whether they use third-party testing to verify security, and how they handle software updates associated with recalls and service campaigns to ensure that these are done securely. The questions specifically asked about vulnerabilities associated with tire pressure monitoring systems, Bluetooth/wireless communications technologies, Onstar/navigation systems, smart phone/mobile device integration, web browsers, electronic control units (ECUs), and vehicle-to-vehicle communication technologies.

Of the 16 automobile manufacturers that responded to the letter, 13 of them addressed these questions in some way. Chrysler, Mercedes-Benz, and Mazda did not respond to the question at all, and five other manufacturers provided general responses that addressed the question as a whole instead of providing specific responses to the questions' sub-parts.

This question seems to have been interpreted differently by different manufacturers. About half of the responses described security or encryption measures for general or specific WEPs that were more related to ensuring the WEPs were working as intended but not to ensuring that a security breach could not occur, and the other half mentioned procedures used in their development process to conduct targeted evaluations of their security measures. The responses revolving around security and encryption measures varied widely from manufacturer to manufacturer, and included the following:

1. Unique identification numbers and specific sets of radio-frequency signals;
2. Receptor to determine frequency strength of sensors to allow for proximity of legitimate communications;
3. Encrypted codes and dedicated wireless devices;
4. Encryption, masking, scanning, anomaly detection, certificates, filtering, firewalls, data loss prevention, access control, intrusion detection systems, white listing, fraud detection, zoning, network segregation and proprietary communication tools;

5. Closed systems where the implementations do not allow the ability for code to be written without authorized tools;
6. Secure Sockets Layer to encrypt the data of network connections;
7. Seed-key security to protect against unauthorized access to the ECU.

Automobile security experts consulted by Senator Markey's staff said that unique ID numbers and radio frequencies (responses 1, 2) can be identified by hackers, that closed system codes (responses 3, 5) have been proven to be re-writable, and seed-key security (response 7) is easily bypassed.

The other half of the responses named procedures utilized in the development process that manufacturers use to ensure WEP security, which was more in line with the wording and intent of the question. These responses included the following steps:

- Threat modeling;
- Penetration testing;
- Input validation and verification;
- Virtual testing;
- Component testing;
- Physical testing.

Seven of the manufacturers stated that they use third-party testing to verify their security measures, while 5 stated that they do not and 4 did not respond to this part of the question.

Automakers were also asked about the number of safety recalls and service campaigns issued by the manufacturers over the five-year period from 2009- 2013 and whether those recalls or service campaigns involved software updates that could be used to introduce malware. Chrysler, Mercedes-Benz, Porsche, and Volkswagen did not respond, with the other 12 companies provided different levels of detail in their responses. The responses ranged from 27-210 combined recall or campaign events during that five-year period, with 11-44% of those including software updates of some kind, all of which were delivered using a hardwire connection (not over-theair like some mobile phone updates are delivered) through a dealer or service center.

The manufacturers were also asked about how they secure this type of software delivery. Each manufacturer responded with descriptions of how they provide such software through authorized dealers with the appropriate tools. Automobile security experts consulted by Senator Markey's staff said that all of the responses are similar in that they presume a malicious actor could not access or acquire the technologies that mechanics have. They state that software updates for systems should be cryptographically verified by the ECU being updated in order to effectively prevent intrusions.

Finding #4: Only two automobile manufacturers were able to describe any capabilities to diagnose or meaningfully respond to an infiltration in real-time, and most say they rely on technologies that cannot be used for this purpose at all.

When asked about how manufacturers are capable of monitoring electronic systems in real-time in order to detect and respond to potential intrusions, most of the responses described systems that can only record information on-board the vehicle. This means that infiltrations would only come to the attention of the manufacturer if that data were manually downloaded by a dealer or service center at some subsequent date. When asked about how they would respond to an infiltration, most manufacturers did not respond or mentioned generic security systems in place. Only two manufacturers described credible real-time reactions to an intrusion event.

The manufacturers were asked whether they include technologies to monitor vehicle CAN buses (the "controller area networks" that manage the communications among the different electronic systems in a vehicle) and to monitor WEPs. They were then asked about how they would respond to reports or detection of an unauthorized intrusion, a remote attack, or inadvertent introduction of malicious code to a WEP. Only eight of sixteen manufacturers responded to these questions, six of which claim to do CAN bus monitoring and five of which claim to be able to detect wireless intrusions. The other 2 manufacturers who responded to the question admitted that they do not monitor the CAN bus, but they are developing systems to do so. Of the other eight companies, Mercedes-Benz, Nissan, and Porsche did not respond at all, and five other manufacturers stated that such information was confidential.

The responses received varied in level of detail and in their methods of monitoring CAN buses. The six manufacturers who claim to monitor CAN buses cited the following:

1. One manufacturer claimed to have a proprietary system that cannot be disclosed;
2. Two manufacturers claimed that the electronic control unit (ECU) is equipped with; monitoring systems that can detect unusual signals, which would alert the manufacturer only if the data were later retrieved at a service center or dealership;

3. One manufacturer described a firewall and watchdog system that shields communication and recognizes inconsistencies at gateways;
4. One manufacturer listed message authentication, intrusion detection, controller hardening protection, secure diagnostics, secure gateways, and secure programming;
5. One manufacturer mentioned that seed-key security is applied to protect vehicles from unauthorized access, which generates a random security variable which must be matched in order to allow communication access.

Automobile security experts consulted by Senator Markey's staff noted that the ECU monitoring (response 2) and firewall/watchdog systems (response 3) would only check for unusual network behavior and not detect any problems with the data itself. An analogy was given to compare it to somebody receiving threatening phone calls, where the phone company is monitoring the lines to see if phone calls are getting through, but not checking the content of the conversations. They also noted that the seed-key system (response 5) could be bypassed by malicious actors.

The question of monitoring WEPs for intrusions received similar responses. Of the eight manufacturers that responded:

1. Four manufacturers mentioned that some of the features themselves are equipped with encryption and security technologies;
2. One manufacturer mentioned continuous ECU monitoring (also above);
3. One manufacturer described the firewall/ watchdog system (also above);
4. One manufacturer described the seed-key security system (also above);
5. One manufacturer stated that its remote keyless entry systems can record key code authentication failures.

The encryption and security measures (response group 1) are not systems that can detect intrusion events. Automobile security experts consulted by Senator Markey's staff have noted that the ECU monitoring (response 2) described simply monitors the normal functioning of an ECU, the firewall/watchdog systems (response 3) would only protect against random outside influences like electromagnetic frequency interference and not malicious intrusions, the seed-key system (response 4) can be defeated by hackers, and the remote keyless entry systems (response 5) will only protect against people getting into the car to steal it but will do nothing to prevent or respond to remote hacking. Also, only 1 of the systems, the seed-key system, is capable of alerting the manufacturer in real-time.

Finally, on the question of how the manufacturers would respond to an intrusion in real-time, six of the manufacturers did not respond, and six more responded with vague mentions of security systems and "taking appropriate actions" such as recalls and service campaigns that could not be used to respond in real-time. The other four manufacturers provided the following responses:

1. One manufacturer claimed that it would contact the subscriber through the telematics program to alert them and resolve any problems;
2. One manufacturer said that it has the ability to disable certain connected features;
3. One manufacturer claimed that it could place a vehicle in a "fail-safe" mode that may limit vehicle operation if malfunctions that could cause damage occur;
4. One manufacturer stated that it would have the option to safely slowdown and immobilize an impacted vehicle if the vehicle is in motion at the time of detection.

The first 2 of these responses, contacting through the telematics program or disabling features, would not be an effective real-time way to deal with an ongoing attack, according to automobile security experts consulted by Senator Markey's staff. Responses 3 and 4, fail-safe mode and remote slowdown and immobilization, are the only responses that indicate an ability to immediately respond to security threats and address the situation for the drivers who subscribe to their telematics providers.

These three questions and their responses have revealed that, of the manufacturers who were willing to respond, only one of them appears to be able to detect wireless intrusions, and only one or two have described credible means of responding to such intrusions in real time.

Finding #5: Automobile manufacturers collect large amounts of data on driving history and vehicle performance.

New vehicles are capable of collecting a tremendous amount of data through a variety of pre-installed technological systems. Senator Markey's letter asked manufacturers about (1) what types of navigation technology or other technologies are in their vehicles with the ability to collect driving history information, (2) what percentage of U.S. automobiles contain such technologies in MY2013 and MY2014, and (3) what types of information can be collected. Honda, Porsche, and Mercedes-Benz did not respond to these questions, and the other 13 manufacturers responded with various levels of completeness.

The responses to the first question included a range of navigation, telematics, infotainment, emergency assist, stolen vehicle recovery, and event data recording systems that have the ability to record driving history information. These included branded products like OnStar and SYNC as well as other unbranded technologies, collecting a diverse set of data types that included the following:

- Geographic location (7 manufacturers), such as:
- Physical location recorded at regular intervals;
- Previous destinations entered into navigation system;
- Last location parked.
- System settings for event data recorder (EDR) devices (5 manufacturers), which can include:
- Potential crash events, such as sudden changes in speed;
- Status of steering angle, brake application, seat belt use, and air bag deployment;
- Fault/error codes in electronic systems.
- Operational data (7 manufacturers), such as:
- Vehicle speed;
- Direction/heading of travel;
- Distances and times traveled;
- Average fuel economy/consumption;
- Status of power windows, doors, and locks;
- Tire pressure;
- Fuel level;
- Tachometer reading (engine RPM gauge);
- Odometer reading;
- Mileage since last oil change;
- Battery health;
- Coolant temperature;
- Engine status;
- Exterior temperature and pressure.

While three of the manufacturers who responded claimed to not record any driving history information, three others listed all three of the categories above.

The percentages of vehicles that contain such technologies varied greatly among the manufacturers, with some claiming that almost no vehicles have them while others claim that all of their vehicle models do. The percentages are shown in the chart below, with a median response of 35% of vehicles from a manufacturer containing technologies that can collect driving history information. These percentages either showed slight increases or stagnation from MY2013-MY2014.

PERCENTAGE OF VEHICLES THAT CAN RECORD DRIVING HISTORY

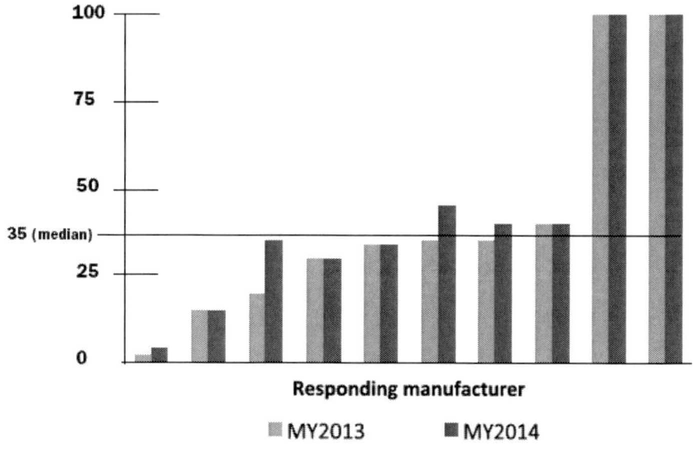

The two coalitions of manufacturers recently adopted voluntary privacy principles — namely on "data minimization, de-identification, and retention" that attempt to address these concerns. On minimization, this principle states that manufacturers commit to collecting information "only as needed for legitimate business purposes." While this is a good step forward, limiting themselves to collection "only as needed for legitimate business purposes" still raises many questions about the extent to which companies will continue to collect sensitive information. The principles also do not ensure that consumers will have rights to prevent data collection in the first place.

Finding #6: A majority of automakers offer technologies that collect and wirelessly transmit driving history data to data centers, including third-party data centers, and most do not describe effective means to secure the data.

Automobile manufacturers store data in a variety of different ways. Some said that it is only stored on-board the vehicle and cannot be wirelessly retrieved, and others described how they wirelessly transfer all data to a central location (known as off-board storage). Also, the large majority of the companies who responded (9 of 11) claimed that they do contract with third-party companies to provide the data-collecting features that they offer. In fact, 3 manufacturers specifically stated they license third party companies to transmit and store data associated with the features.

To the question of whether driving history information is recorded and stored in a vehicle, 12 manufacturers replied that they do store this information in some of their vehicles (depending on the features the vehicle is equipped with). Only 1 manufacturer stated that they do not collect such data, and 3 did not respond. This indicates that an overwhelming majority of vehicles collect driving history information.

Of the 12 who said they collect and store driving history data, 8 stated that they transmit and store driving history data in a server off-board the vehicle, while the other 4 stated that they do not. This reveals that a majority of vehicle manufacturers offer features that not only record but also transmit driving history wirelessly to themselves or to third parties.

PERCENTAGE OF AUTOMOBILE MANUFACTURERS THAT COLLECT AND TRANSMIT DRIVING HISTORY DATA

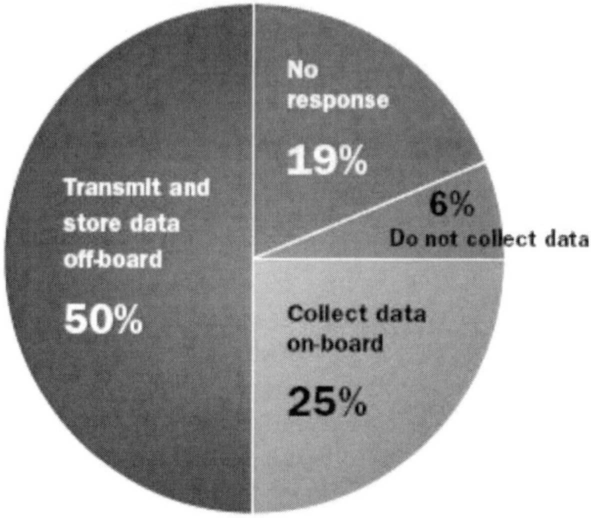

Finally, the security measures of these data collection systems vary widely by manufacturer, and in some cases there are none. In the case of on-board storage, no manufacturer described any security system to protect that data, and several of them noted that no security measure is needed since accessing data would require a hardwire connection. Regarding security measures to protect data that is wirelessly transmitted outside the vehicle, only 6 responses were received. Of those, 5 provided vague responses naming encryption, passwords, or general IT security practices, and only 1 specifically mentioned that they designed their systems to limit the transfer of personally identifiable information.

The automakers' voluntary privacy protection principles include commitments to "respect for context" and "data security." The "respect for context" principle addresses the ways that data are collected and shared, and it provides a list of examples to illustrate "reasonable and responsible ways" that automakers may collect and share data with both affiliated companies and non-affiliated entities. These include, among others, providing subscribed services, conducting research, responding to emergencies and faults, sharing for operational purposes, and complying with lawful government requests — describing a sweeping suite of practices and offering no specific guidelines for reducing data collection and sharing.

The "data security" principle states that the automakers commit to collecting information "only as needed for legitimate business purposes," which is another positive message toward reducing unneeded sharing of information. However, this principle offers no detail as to what may be included under "legitimate business purposes," effectively leaving it open for interpretation by the coalition members.

Finding #7: Manufacturers use personal vehicle data in various ways, often vaguely to "improve the customer experience" and usually involving third parties, and retention policies — how long they store information about drivers — vary considerably among manufacturers.

A wide array of responses was received regarding the ways that manufacturers use vehicle history information. Of the 8 manufacturers that previously stated that they collect such information, 3 of them did not respond to this question, with the other five listing combinations of the following uses:

- Provide feature functionality;
- Maintain and improve services;
- Address vehicle safety concerns;
- Diagnose and assist with technical issues;
- Respond when the system senses the vehicle has been involved in an accident;
- Fulfill requests for service by customers;
- Research purposes (analytics and marketing).

Many of these responses are vague and not well-defined, such as providing feature functionality, maintaining and improving services, and serving research purposes. This lack of transparency in personal vehicle data usage leaves consumers with little knowledge about how the companies actually use their data.

Additionally, the letters revealed that 5 of the 8 manufacturers claimed to share this information with third parties to provide subscriber services. All of them stated that they do not sell such information, and 2 specifically mentioned that they do not share any personally identifiable information. This reveals that a majority of manufacturers who collect data share that information with third party companies.

Another question that received a wide range of responses was about how long driving history data is retained in the various systems that record and store them. To this question, four of the twelve manufacturers did not answer, with the other eight providing responses that sometimes varied by feature/technology. These ranged from responses that information is retained no longer than a year, to responses that indicate that information is retained indefinitely.

- Five manufacturers listed that information is deleted after a set period of time, ranging from one to ten years;
- Three manufacturers replied that there is no set clear date, with two of them stating that it can be deleted by users at any time;
- One manufacturer stated that navigation information is overwritten when the system runs out of memory storage space;
- One manufacturer said that on-board error information is deleted when the vehicle fault is cleared.

The new industry-led voluntary privacy principles include a commitment by automakers to only collect data "as needed for legitimate business purposes" and to retain identifiable or personal subscription information "no longer than they determine necessary for legitimate business purposes." The intention of this principle is positive, but these limitations are subject to the interpretation of the industry and offer no explicit rules to prevent excessive collection or retention. Regarding the ways in which data are used, the coalitions put forth the "respect for context" principle, which describes a list of "reasonable and responsible ways" that members can use or share data collected from vehicles. This includes an important provision that a warrant or court order is needed if companies are to share geolocation information with law enforcement. Unfortunately, however, this broad proclamation provides little tangible assurances that consumers will not disapprove of the ways in which manufacturers use their sensitive information.

Additionally, the automakers' voluntary "choice" principle specifically requires affirmative consent from the consumer before sharing sensitive driving history data, specifically geolocation, biometric, and driver behavior information, for marketing purposes or with unaffiliated third parties. However, this commitment fails to address whether a consumer's decision to agree or disagree will affect the functionality of the vehicle or the features that are available to them. The principles also do not pertain to sharing

1) non-sensitive data for marketing purposes, and
2) sensitive data for non-marketing purposes.

Finding #8: Customers are often not explicitly made aware of data collection and, when they are, they often cannot opt out without disabling valuable features, such as navigation.

The primary methods manufacturers use to inform customers of data collection are by mentioning it in the owners' manual or including it in the terms and conditions of the vehicle sale or specific feature activation. If a customer actually becomes aware of data collection and wishes to disable it, they often must accept a loss of feature functionality, such as GPS.

Of the twelve manufacturers who confirmed that they do record and store data, three did not respond to the question on how customers are made aware of data storage, and one stated that there is no reason to inform users of on-board storage. The other eight manufacturers listed combinations of the following methods of notice:

- Owners' manuals; ¡ Privacy statements;
- Terms & Conditions (which must be "accepted").

To the question of whether and how customers can disable data collection or transmission, four did not respond. Two manufacturers said that users cannot disable data collection, two said that they can disable it, and four stated that it is possible by turning off a feature or canceling a service subscription.

On the question of whether users (if they are made aware of data collection) can delete information, six manufacturers did not respond, five specifically noted that customers can delete data directly through the navigation system interface, and one mentioned that customers can request data deletion by contacting the service provider.

These responses show that customer awareness of data collection is primarily distributed within long written texts such as Terms & Agreement statements or owner manuals. In the event that customers read these and are aware of them, they do, in certain cases, have the ability to delete previously-recorded data. However, disabling the constant collection of data often requires disabling valuable vehicle features or services.

The new voluntary privacy principles from the manufacturers partially address these concerns with commitments to "transparency" and "choice." Signing members agree to provide consumers "with ready access to clear, meaningful notices about the Participating Member's collection, use, and sharing" of data. This includes a list of ways that manufacturers can provide these notices, which include "owners' manuals, on paper or electronic registration forms and user agreements, or on in-vehicle displays."

Unfortunately, these types of notices likely do not guarantee an improvement over current practices revealed in the responses to Senator Markey, as most manufacturers claimed that such notices are already provided in user manuals and terms & conditions that must be signed upon purchase.

Regarding choice, the principle states that consumers must give "affirmative consent," or opt in, when certain information such as geolocation, biometrics, or driver behavior is collected or shared for marketing or with unaffiliated third parties. The principle does not commit manufacturers to offering consumers the option to prevent data collection in the first place or giving consumers the choice to remove data that have already been collected. Additionally, consumers who choose not to consent to data collection may be denied access to valuable vehicle features. For instance, consent to sharing geolocation information for marketing purposes may be the only way for a consumer to turn on the navigation feature.

End Notes

[1] http://www.markey.senate.gov/news/press-releases/as-wireless-technology-becomes-standard-markey-queries-carcompanies-about-security-privacy.

[2] "Adventures in Automotive Networks and Control Units," Dr. Charlie Miller and Chris Valasek, http://illmatics.com/car_hacking.pdf.

[3] http://www.npr.org/blogs/alltechconsidered/2013/07/30/206800198/Smarter-Cars-Open-New-Doors-To-Smarter-Thieves

[4] "Black Hat 2014: Hacking the Smart Car," Mark Anderson, IEEE Spectrum, http://spectrum.ieee.org/cars-that-think/transportation/systems/black-hat-2014-hacking-the-smart-car.

[5] See "Researchers Show How a Car's Electronics Can Be Taken Over Remotely," John Markoff, The New York Times, March 9, 2011, http://www.nytimes.com/2011/03/10/ business/10hack.html http://www.autosec.org/pubs/cars-oakland2010.pdf and http://www.autosec.org/pubs/cars-usenixsec2011.pdf.

[6] "Dash is Turning Cars into Futurists, Data-Collecting Machines with an App and a Cheap Plastic Dongle," Alyson Shontell, Business Insider, http://www.businessinsider.com/a-tiny-piece-of-hardware-turns-your-vehicle-into-a- smart-car-that-talks-and-collect-tons-of-data-2013-8.

[7] See "Elon Musk's Data Doesn't Back Up His Claims of New York Times Fakery," Rebecca Greenfield, The Atlantic Wire, http://www.theatlanticwire.com/technology/2013/02/elon-musks-data-doesnt-back-his-claims-new-york-times-fakery/62149/and http://www.teslamotors.com/blog/most-peculiar-test-drive.

[8] "Late on a Car Loan? Meet the Disabler," Jonathan Welsh, The Wall Street Journal, http://online.wsj.com/article/SB123794137545832713.html,

[9] Vehicle-to-Vehicle Technologies Expected to Offer Safety Benefits, but a Variety of Deployment Challenges Exist," Government Accountability Office, GAO-14-13, http://www.gao.gov/assets/660/658709.pdf.

[10] "Consumer Privacy Protection Principles, Alliance of Automobile Manufacturers, Inc. and Association of Global Automakers, Inc., November 12, 2014, http://www.autoalliance.org/index.cfm?objectid=CC629950-6A96-11E4-866D000C296BA163.

[11] "Researchers Show How a Car's Electronics Can Be Taken Over Remotely," John Markoff, The New York Times, March 9, 2011, http://www.nytimes.com/2011/03/10/business/10hack.html.

INDEX

A

B

C

F

G

H

I

L

M

N

S

T

U

V

W